Lincoln Christian College

talks for children
on science and God

# talks
# for children
# on science
# and God

## GRAHAM R. HODGES

⚹

### ABINGDON PRESS
NEW YORK · NASHVILLE

TALKS FOR CHILDREN ON SCIENCE AND GOD

Library of Congress Catalog Card Number: 64-21131

"Steering by the Stars," "The Good
Earth," and "How Much Can We Know?"
previously appeared in *Pulpit Digest*.

SET UP, PRINTED, AND BOUND BY THE
PARTHENON    PRESS,    AT    NASHVILLE,
TENNESSEE, UNITED STATES OF AMERICA

to Elsie

# foreword

I have several hobbies, none of them very glamorous and certainly none are moneymaking.

One is the reading of new books, which are constantly being published, in the many, many fields of science. They are so many that no man could read them all even if he spent twenty-four hours a day at it.

But I enjoy trying to read them. Not being a scientist, much of what I read is over my head, especially the technical parts containing mathematics.

I especially like science books containing illustrative photographs or drawings. For example, almost every week there appears a new book on astronomy and space. For the most part these are very complicated books. But I check them out of our local library and read what parts I can understand. If there are photos of the distant galaxies I pore over them, spending many minutes gazing at these marvelous pictures of vast star clouds like our own Milky Way, each containing billions of stars. I like to ponder about how and if man could ever reach them, whether there are earths like our own, and if there are people like us there with the same kind of joy, pain, and pleasure, and whether they die like us or have they discovered a way of living forever.

Likewise I like to read science books about the Arctic and Antarctic regions. So many good ones, well illustrated, are published today. How interesting to read of the two-mile-thick layer of ice at the South Pole, and how its weight has pressed a high plateau down to sea level.

Another science-book hobby is the study of geology and the formation of rocks, mountains, plains, oil, and coal. Another fascinating kind of book deals with dinosaurs. Did you know that the dinosaur, with his dozens of kinds, ruled the earth supreme for about 100,000,000 years? Longer by far than man has.

Another interesting reading area for me is the virus field. How entertaining to read about these smallest of living things. Are they plants, animals, or mere specks of matter which reproduce themselves and are capable of causing diseases in plants, animals, and human beings?

The fact that I understand so little doesn't prevent my enjoying books about science. It has been my hobby since I studied physics, chemistry, and biology in high school and college.

Yes, these are science books I read. But they are also books about God, about religion, about the doings of our Creator, our Heavenly Father, just as much as any part of the Bible. For anything which describes God is about religion. And our puny efforts to tell about the universe and nature in our new books on science's many different fields of study are nothing but attempts to understand the way God works. We may call it science. I call it God and his hidden secrets.

When I read about the unbelievable migrations of birds and fishes, the vast distances and the thinness of space, the trillions of stars, the heat of the sun's interior —then, to me, I am reading about God and marveling all the more at how wonderful he is.

If the ancient psalmist were writing today, he might not write at all. For he knew so little, compared to us, about the universe. If he knew what we know he might be made speechless in trying to describe God.

Read books on science. That's a wonderful way to learn about God.

GRAHAM R. HODGES

# contents

# science and religion—
## the questions they ask

Ask, and it will be given you; seek and you will find; knock and it will be opened to you.—Matt. 7:7

We are always disappointed when we ask a question of somebody who can't possibly answer it. For example, to find out how much it costs to mail a ten-pound parcel of sugar to San Francisco or Chicago, we don't ask the corner grocer. It's not his business to know. We ask the postmaster.

And this holds true in the more important questions of life. Much disappointment and even anger can come if we ask the wrong questions in the wrong places.

This has happened to many boys and girls who have asked of the church and religion questions which they should refer to their science teacher or to an encyclopedia. On the other hand, they are frequently disappointed when they try to find in their science books questions best answered through Bible reading, prayer, church attendance, or a talk with a friendly, older Christian person.

Science asks and tries to answer such questions as

these: How heavy, or soft, or long, or wide is an object? What is its chemical composition? How is it made or destroyed? How is a machine constructed? How does it operate? What is its best fuel? What kind of plant or animal is this? What are its diseases and how are they cured? How many stars are there and how far away? What theories explain mysteries of nature we don't understand?

On the other hand, religion, or our ideas about man and God, tries to answer such questions as these: Who am I? Who made me? Do I have a soul? Where does it go when I die? How can I be a better person? What is life? What is death? What is right, and what is wrong? How can I do right and avoid wrong? What causes suffering? What is success, and what is failure? Where is the human race going? Should we use the atom bomb in war? How can we love those who hate or mistreat us?

You see, science and religion both have more questions than they can answer. They are partners working together to find answers we all want, not enemies trying to give opposite answers to the same questions.

Of course, there are times when those who call themselves scientists try to live without God and also religious persons who try to live without the truth revealed to man through science. But the attempt, either way, does not last long, though sometimes bitter things are said. It took the church many years to accept Galileo's discovery that the sun, not the earth, was the center of the solar system. Now we live quite happily knowing that our ancestors, for thousands of years, were dead wrong thinking the earth was the center of everything.

16

Meanwhile, the great questions of religion continue to challenge each new individual and each new generation.

And as the questions and answers which come from science grow ever larger, the more we need the answers which only religion can provide. The more answers science gives, the greater grows our need for religion and God.

# *the flight of the phoebe*

Whither shall I go from thy Spirit?
  Or whither shall I flee from thy presence?
If I ascend to heaven, thou art there!
  If I make my bed in Sheol, thou art there!
If I take the wings of the morning
  and dwell in the uttermost parts of the sea,
Even there thy hand shall lead me,
  and thy right hand shall hold me.—Ps. 139:7-10

What is a phoebe? It is a small bird commonly found all over the eastern United States in the summer. It most frequently builds its nest, made of mud and grass, around barns, houses in the woods, and old buildings.

The phoebe, so called because it says fee-be, fee-be, fee-be, flits its tail right and left, up and down, as it sits on a branch, frequently near a stream. For a phoebe to eat several hundred insects a day is nothing at all.

17

Since it does eat an enormous number of insects, it is a good friend of the farmer and gardener.

Like many other birds, the tiny phoebe can do wonderful things we human beings cannot understand nor can the phoebe itself, I presume.

When it leaves in the fall for its winter home on the Gulf Coast or in Mexico, Mr. and Mrs. Phoebe separate. Instead of going together they bid each other good-bye in their phoebe language, then join other phoebes flying south.

But the good-bye is not final. Several weeks later they meet, many hundreds of miles southward, in their permanent winter home, whether that be in Mexico or in our own Gulf states.

And in the spring, when they fly back north, they do the same thing all over again, flying separately and meeting exactly at their old nesting place of the previous year. Unless one dies or is killed on the journey, they never fail to meet—Mr. and Mrs. Phoebe. Often they repair and use again the same nest they used the year before.

How do they do it? Scientists don't know. Somehow God has given to the phoebe this mysterious power of traveling nearly two thousand miles and meeting at an exact spot without fail.

Other birds, too, have a similar power. A group of starlings have called my garage attic "home" for many years. Each spring finds them back at their old stand, after a winter in the South.

We human beings are so impressed with what we call "manmade miracles," such as rocket ships, radio,

18

television, and electronic computers, that we seldom think about the great miracles of nature which have been here all these thousands of years. Long before Columbus discovered America, the phoebe family was flying northward and southward each year, always meeting at a prearranged spot.

Our lives are richer, fuller, and more contented if we turn our minds each day to God's wonders. Such a practice makes us complain less of our troubles. We can worship God more easily if we reflect on his powers and how he provides for his animal children as well as for his human children.

Because so many of us live in cities with little contact with nature, we must deliberately learn all we can by reading as well as watching. Each new fact about the world of nature is a new fact about God.

How do Mr. and Mrs. Phoebe always meet at the right spot? I don't know, but God does.

# *fingerprints*

Why, even the hairs of your head are all numbered.
—Luke 12:7

God's power to create an infinite, or numberless, kind and variety of differences in living things is only one of his amazing and delightfully surprising wonders.

Nowhere is this power shown more clearly or closely than right on the last joint of your fingers and thumbs. Yes, your fingerprints.

Look at them carefully and well. On each of your ten fingers including the two thumbs—for they are fingers, too—are tiny ridges arranged in a pattern which is different from any other arrangement ever seen on any finger belonging to any of the billions and billions of people over thousands of years past and which is different from any in the present.

Like many other commonplace facts clear as the nose on your face or in this case the fingers of your hand, nobody realized that all fingerprints are different from all other fingerprints until quite recently in history.

Less than a hundred years ago police experts in England, France, and America discovered that we can be identified absolutely by our fingerprint arrangements and a system of classification was developed. So today in Washington, D.C., the Federal Bureau of Investigation has on record many millions of fingerprint sets. By a phone call your local police can find out in a few moments from the F.B.I. in Washington to whom such and such a set of fingerprints belongs. All fingerprints belong to one of four groups: the arch, the loop, the whorl, and the composite. By counting the numbers of ridges in these arches, loops, whorls, and composites fingerprint experts can quickly describe fingerprints by telephone or telegraph. Not even a photograph of the prints is needed. It can all be done with classifications and codes.

Study your own fingerprints and your friends' and you

will see very clearly these arrangements of tiny ridges. It's best done with an ordinary magnifying glass or reading glass.

This unending variety of creation extends to our feet, also. The footprints of newborn babies are put on their birth certificates in all our hospitals today. Why? Because no two footprints are alike either, and the pattern of each individual will remain the same as long as he lives.

Our ears are all different, too. No two sets of ears are any more identical than any two sets of fingerprints or footprints.

Again, there is no human face exactly like any other human face, even in identical twins. Going further, the same applies to our arms, legs, and all parts of us.

Perhaps this endless variety in nature, with no two living things alike, does not impress you. Ho, hum, you may say. So what is so important about that?

But it is important and it is amazing. If you and I had the job of arranging all the fingerprints, faces, ears, legs, arms, hairs, and all the other parts of each newborn babe, we would get so tired of the job that by about the one-thousandth baby we would say, "Let's make them all alike!" And what a dreadful world *that* would make.

But God doesn't get tired. Day after day, year after year, century after century each human being and each animal is created anew, different from any other before or since—all originals. No copies, please, with him.

Look at your fingerprints. Then look at the stars. God put equal and loving care on them both.

21

Aren't you glad that he just doesn't stamp us all out of a machine, like so many bottlecaps or paper clips?

# light from the nearest star

The heavens are telling the glory of God;
    and the firmament proclaims his handiwork.
Day to day pours forth speech,
    and night to night declares knowledge.—Ps. 19:1-2

Have you ever tried to work or read or sew or walk by starlight? Pretty difficult or impossible isn't it? That is, if you try by the starlight at night.

But in the day it's a different matter. Then starlight literally floods the earth, even on the cloudiest day. For starlight is sunlight and sunlight is starlight.

Yes, the sun is a star, the nearest star to us. It is our personal star. And sunlight so fills our earth that even in the shadows or shade we have enough light for any practical purpose. If you really want to know what true starlight is, go outside any day and look at the landscape and sky. You can't find any spot where starlight isn't shining or reflecting.

In the day sunlight floods every nook and cranny, giving life to all plants and animals, making life possible for us. The sun makes trees and grass grow, rains fall and rivers flow, tides rise, winds blow, and life flourish everywhere.

22

The next nearest star is Alpha Centauri, 4.3 light years or many trillions of miles away. Its light isn't strong enough for any practical purpose here.

It is strange how we forget that starlight floods half the earth all the time, but no stranger than the way we forget the presence of God's love which is everywhere, at all times, in all situations.

When we think of how God shows himself, we imagine we must use examples from the Bible or of missionaries in Africa or of sermons in the church. This is like looking for starlight at night.

A better way is to find a place or time or situation where God's great love doesn't exist. This would be impossible, for every time I think, breathe, eat, walk, talk, or sleep I am using gifts from God and so are you. His presence and power are everywhere—just like the sunlight. Even when we can't see his love directly, we see it reflected in people's lives and in nature. Why do we try to find him in the darkness when he is everywhere in the light?

We don't need a telescope to see God—just plain commonsense and open eyes. We don't have to be experts in astronomy or religion—just ordinary human beings willing to see our Father's loving care.

In thousands of ways every day God's concern for us shows through. The apostle Paul said: "In him we live and move and have our being." Truer words were never written.

Light from the nearest star? It's all around every day, so bright that we can't look directly into it, no more than the mind can understand God's great ways.

23

# science and religion—enemies or partners?

You will know the truth, and the truth will make you free.—John 8:32

Are science and religion enemies? Is it possible to believe in God and Jesus Christ as we read of them in the Bible and still be modern, scientific persons? Does unspoken prayer to an invisible God we have never seen face to face make sense? As we learn more of nature, will our churches become unnecessary?

Not long ago many people thought it was impossible to be a believing Christian and a learned scientist all at once. This view is now out-of-date, for many of our most brilliant scientists are faithful church members.

Instead of being enemies working against each other I would choose to call science and religion partners, working with each other to find the truth, whatever it might be. Might we not compare them with the thumb and fingers of the hand, both parts of the same hand working together to grasp the truth?

The thumb is the most indispensable part of the hand. Remove it and the fingers are far less useful. So religion, or belief in God, is more important than any single science. Let's call religion the thumb.

The fingers may be called by names of various branches of science: geology, zoology, botany, astronomy, paleontology, archaeology, oceanography, physics, and all-important mathematics which is a tool of every science.

The thumb and fingers need one another, so in the same manner do religion and the sciences. Together they grasp at truth. Remove any one, especially the thumb, and the hand cannot do its work well.

Any new discovery of science is a new revelation of God's truth, proving even more his power and love, aiding in man's search for him.

Sciences change very rapidly; religion, slowly, for its beliefs are timeless, depending more on man's inner seeking and not on test tubes, microscopes, or telescopes. And the inner life of man has not changed much these thousands of years.

So the basic beliefs of religion change slowly. Their slow change gives us something permanent to fall back on in times of great needs. If our ideas of God changed as often as our ideas about science, most of us would feel very unsure of God indeed.

Together religion and science, thumb and fingers, may work marvels in bettering the life of man, giving his life meaning, finding new ways for him to help his brother, new avenues to our common God.

Enemies or partners? I believe they can be partners, for they are both part of the same hand and must work together.

# God made the fossils

Of old thou didst lay the foundation of the earth,
and the heavens are the work of thy hands.
They will perish, but thou dost endure.—Ps. 102:25-26

In my hand I hold pieces of limestone. For millions or tens of millions of years the ocean covered the area where this limestone was formed. Countless trillions of sea animals died, leaving their skeletons or shells on the ocean floor, piling layer on layer as the eons passed. Seas rose and fell. Ages followed succeeding ages. The dinosaur reigned supreme over land and sea, then passed away. Ice ages came and went as climates changed.

But still the seas continued to rise, cover, recede, rise, cover, and recede in the area where I found this limestone. Skeletons of animals continued to fall like a slow rain on the ocean floor. Some were microscopic, too small to be seen by the human eye. Some were larger, such as oysters, clams, mussels, and all their relatives.

Examine any piece of limestone with the naked eye or magnifying glass and more than likely you will see embedded there these skeletons. Many of them represent animals long ago extinct, all dead long before man came to earth.

Not even the warm-blooded creatures who preceded man on earth were around when most of this limestone was formed at the ocean's bottom. As yet no horses, cats, chickens, cows, or songbirds had appeared. Not a single house had been built or road laid or city erected. The world was a different place, indeed.

The world was inhabited entirely by creatures we know today mainly by study of their fossils.

But there was One living then, as well as now. He was the Creator of this world—God. It was God's world then just as it is now, and he was the same God.

He was creating, changing, rearranging, getting it ready for his children whom we call "human beings." Finally, when the world was ready, no sooner and no later, he created man—men and women, boys and girls.

How marvelous is the thought that God was here running the world when these limestone fossils were living sea creatures!

Perhaps he had us in mind when he created this very stone, thinking of our needs for buildings, roads, and homes constructed from it.

To me it brings great comfort to know that the same God who helped make this limestone eons ago is still right here on this same spot caring for his human children. Such a dependable God, you can trust. He is not here today and gone tomorrow, but he is always, ever, and forever the same, loving, and reliable God.

This is the God Jesus came to reveal to us, the God the psalmist was thinking of when he wrote the words at the top of this talk, the same God who is with you and me when we say at night: "Now I lay me down to sleep."

# what holds the earth up?

*He stretches out the north over the void,*
*and hangs the earth upon nothing.—Job 26:7*

What holds the earth up? What keeps such an enormous weight from falling into nothingness?

Men have wondered about this for a long time and have come up with some very queer answers indeed. The ancient Greeks, wise though they were, imagined that an immense giant named Atlas bore the earth forever on his shoulders as punishment for wrongdoing. Hence, *Atlas* to us means strength.

The ancient Hebrews believed that the earth floated upon "the great deep," a huge sea which not only bore up the land areas of the world, but also covered the sky above. Another ancient religion, that of the Norsemen, had this same idea, that the earth was floating on a great sea. What held up the sea? Nobody knew.

An old Hindu myth has it that a god turned himself into a giant tortoise and balanced the earth on his back.

However farfetched such explanations seem to us, we must admit that these, our ancestors, did at least wonder about the matter and arrived at the best explanation they could. To think that water surrounded and supported the land was certainly natural, as everywhere men traveled water finally met land, and nobody had ever sailed to the ocean's end. Not until Columbus discovered America was it actually proved that the earth was round.

Strangely enough, the Book of Job, saying that God

"hangs the earth upon nothing," comes close to the actual scientific fact that an invisible force called *gravity* really holds up the earth.

We have all twirled objects around our heads on the end of a string. The spinning force holds up the object. Likewise our earth is spinning around the sun, held at an exact distance away by the force of its attraction to the sun and the force which would make it spin straight out into space. All the planets are held up by just such a force as this.

And what holds up the solar system composed of the sun and its planets? Again, the whole system is spinning merrily away in space around a huge galaxy of stars, the Milky Way, which, in turn, is held by gravity to other galaxies.

So, as far as any holding up is concerned, the writer of the Book of Job is exactly right, God hangs the earth upon nothing we can see.

The Bible tells us "with God all things are possible." So he holds the earth—without its being touched at any point—out in thin space, spinning round the sun and, in turn, moving around the center of the Milky Way.

The whole system of stars, holding one another up in empty space while trillions of miles apart, is so fantastic and unbelievable to the human mind that it is almost simpler to go back to poor old Atlas or the giant tortoise. But these stories weren't true, so we modern people turn to explanations which fit the facts.

What holds up the earth? God, through the laws of the universe.

29

# what and where is heaven?

When I go and prepare a place for you, I will come again
and take you to myself.—John 14:3

An airplane crashes and eighty passengers and crew
members die suddenly. A ship sinks and several hundred
persons drown. Five persons are killed instantly when a
car crashes. Is this the end of these people? If not, what
happens to them?

A very dear friend or relative dies at home or in the
local hospital. Is their death the last of these friends or
loved ones?

Some say, "Yes, that is all. When death comes that is
the end of us. Since the body is all we can see, then we
can't prove there is a soul inside to continue living."

Yes, it is difficult or almost impossible to prove scientifically that there is something more to each of us than
the physical body which moves about, eats food, sleeps,
suffers pain, goes to sleep each night, and finally ceases
to live because of old age, accident, or illness. As a minis-
ter I have been present at the death of many persons and
can honestly say I have never seen a soul leave the body.

But neither have I ever seen love, hate, beauty, fear,
gratitude, or joy. But they exist. I have never seen Jesus.
But I know he lives. I have never seen God. But he
exists just the same. I have never seen gravity. I know
it is a force in operation nevertheless.

What happens when we die? Where does our soul, that
invisible part of us, go?

Actually, we are not sure. But we are sure that Jesus will be wherever we go to welcome us.

But where will this be? Where is the heaven which Jesus spoke so much about and which we learn of in Sunday school and church?

Is it a place? Or a country? Or a city? Or just a lot of beautiful houses with lovely trees, parks, meadows, and fields all over? Will the houses be of gold with diamonds for windows?

If anybody has seen it, why don't we have pictures of heaven as we do of the moon and sun? Why didn't Jesus provide us with some actual scenes from heaven?

All these questions used to come to my mind as a child, and some still do. But the older I get the gladder I am that Jesus was very vague about what wonderful things await us beyond death, when our souls go from our bodies.

Suppose he had told us. It would be too wonderful for us to believe and many would say: "Ugh! Just fairy tales. How could anybody in his right mind believe *that?*"

Or, if he had, there would be no surprise left. If your parents allowed you to open your Christmas presents just any old time, what a dull morning you would have on December 25. You really don't want to know ahead, do you?

So, what waits for us when we die is like getting up to a wonderful Christmas morning.

Jesus wants us to love and obey him here on earth not for reward but because we love him and want to do right in our hearts.

Those who do have Jesus' personal promise that some-

31

where he has prepared a place of great beauty and joy for them to live forever and ever.

## *science says*——

> For our knowledge is imperfect. . . . For now we see in a mirror dimly, but then face to face. Now I know in part; then I shall understand fully, even as I have been fully understood.—I Cor. 13:9, 12

You and I are living in a day when "science" seems to have all the correct answers. If we can say, when arguing a point, that "science says" this or that in our favor, we have half won the argument already.

Advertisements in magazines, newspapers, radio, and television use such phrases as "leading scientists say" or "according to scientists."

Although we must admit that scientific discoveries have brought us a thousand and one blessings, a true scientist would be the first to say that there is no single, final authority on any scientific subject. A true scientist would also be the first to admit that scientific ideas accepted this year may be proved false next year, that we know only a tiny part of the truth about any subject, and that new discoveries may change our ideas about vast areas of nature. In fact, these very things are happening all the time and will continue to happen. Thus, a true scientist does not have the absolute trust in present knowledge which many of us have.

For thousands of years mankind believed that the world was flat, had four corners, and that the sun went around it. All the evidence pointed that way. It looked flat. The sun rose and the sun set.

Only yesterday, as man's history goes, and after great persecution of those who taught our present ideas, such as Galileo, Kepler, and Copernicus, did we change our notions on this important idea. Yet for many centuries our ancestors had said "science says the world is flat and the sun goes round it."

Another notion long held was that there were four elements composing all matter or "stuff": fire, earth, air, and water. "Science" said so.

Until recently nearly all scientists refused to believe that tiny, microscopic organisms we now call germs could cause diseases. The man who proved this fact, Louis Pasteur, was ridiculed and persecuted by most of the leading scientists of his beloved nation, France. This was less than one hundred years ago. You see, science didn't believe in germs.

Science also said atoms couldn't be split. How false that notion was.

Until World War II the medical doctors required their patients to lie in bed for days or weeks even after minor operations. Then experiments proved that people get well much faster and better if they are forced to get out of bed as soon as possible, frequently the next day after the operation. Here is a case of science being open-

33

minded and reversing its opinion on the basis of new facts.

Today many scientists disagree on what is true about certain ideas. What causes cancer? Within a few years we shall probably know. Right now we don't.

Is the universe running down? Is it burning itself out? Is it exploding, staying about the same, or swelling and contracting in cycles? Our smartest scientists are not in agreement on these questions.

A Christian knows that some things never change. God's truth, mercy, forgiveness, and love are eternal. The teachings of Jesus will never change. Why? Because they are revealed or given by God, who knows all.

In contrast, our scientific ideas change as our amount of previous knowledge increases and as our instruments for studying the universe get better. Who could have guessed, before our large one hundred- and two hundred-inch telescopes were made, that there are billions of galaxies, or star clouds, in the universe and, likely, many earths similar to ours? Therefore scientific ideas will constantly change as mankind learns more and more. This will never cease.

So, instead of saying, "science says," we might say, "this is what we think now on the basis of what we know."

God's truth never changes. Jesus' truth never changes. But our ideas about their universe, which we call science, will change more and more.

# God and our genes

For thou didst form my inward parts,
   thou didst knit me together in my mother's womb.
I praise thee, for thou art fearful and wonderful.
Wonderful are thy works!—Ps. 139:13-14

Here is a pattern for making a dress. Here is a blueprint for building a home. Here are directions for making a birdhouse.

But where is the pattern or blueprint or set of directions for making a living thing, such as a plant, an animal, or a human being?

Until about one hundred years ago man had no idea how the human likeness is passed on from generation to generation. How does a pine tree, through its seed, reproduce pine trees instead of oak, elm, or maple? How does a cow have a little calf which becomes another cow? How is it that a calf will have horns, four legs, split hooves, and all the rest of the regular parts of a calf? How is it that human babies have two legs, two arms, one head, two ears, two eyes either blue, brown, black, or hazel instead of purple, one nose with two nostrils, two cheeks, thirty-two teeth, and so on?

If you really think about it for a moment, no kind of accidental arrangement could put together as intricate and wonderful thing as the human body. But until recently we had no idea about the system nature, or God, has provided so that all plants, animals, and human beings can reproduce plants, animals, and human beings like themselves.

35

Then about a hundred years ago an Austrian monk named Gregor J. Mendel, experimenting with the pea plant, discovered that heredity, or the passing on of life from one generation to another, is controlled and determined by microscopic things hitherto unknown called genes. When the female egg and the male sperm of plants and animals combine their genes, each male gene for a certain part of the body or plant, atuomatically, in God's mysterious way, matches up with the right female gene.

For example, the color of your eyes is determined by the genes of your mother and father, and how they combined. The color of skin is passed on the same way; the shape and size of your nose, the same way. I have a large nose—the Hodges nose. For generations back the Hodges family has had an ample nose—always passed along through the genes.

In like manner all the thousands and millions of different possibilities for right and wrong arrangements in babies are determined by genes. Every organ, every blood vessel, the more or less two billion brain cells, the heart, tongue—all the rest, their shape, size, color, consistency, placement, and connections—are determined by our genes. That is why atomic scientists say an atomic war might ruin the human race; exploding atoms could dislocate the human genes and produce a race of abnormal people with many blind, deaf, dumb, mentally defective, or other terrible handicaps. It is a dangerous thing to tamper with God's plan for reproducing ourselves.

We know a vast amount about the genes today. But

there is more to learn than we already know, as is the case in most sciences.

The work of the genes, whether in plants, animals, or human beings, is so wonderful that only an all-powerful God could have conceived and planned them.

No wonder the Psalmist of olden times said:

> Such knowledge is too wonderful for me;
> it is high, I cannot attain it.

# *how does the eel know?*

This is God,
our God for ever and ever.
He will be our guide for ever.
—Ps. 48:14

One of nature's deepest mysteries is the way in which the fish eel finds its way as a tiny larva less than an inch long down under two miles of Atlantic Ocean water to the fresh water streams of Europe and eastern North America, and years later as an adult eel, back to his deep Atlantic birthplace again.

Somehow God has provided this animal with a guiding mechanism which has as yet defied man's explanation. The facts about the eel's travels are these: Each spring there arrives at the river mouths of the Atlantic Ocean an enormous number (millions) of little eels, bright as glass, and about the shape and size of a wooden match. They go up the rivers, and then seek out the farthermost creeks, rills, and ditches connected with these rivers.

In their journey inland they climb over rocks, wriggle up rapids, and slither over damp moss. Nothing stops them. Most of these are female eels. The males remain at the rivers' mouths.

Five years later, the males now about eighteen inches long and the females up to four feet, both changed from a yellowish to silver color, all head homeward, for they are true creatures of the sea though most of their lives are lived in fresh water. Seaward they turn, again stopping at no barrier. They will even wriggle over dewy meadows at night to escape dead-end ditches.

Straight home they head to ocean depths northward and eastward of Puerto Rico. From all over Europe and America they come. There in the deep salty waters they breed, lay their eggs, and die. No eel ever makes the trip inland a second time.

When the eels hatch they are tiny worms. For three years those whose parents came from Europe slowly swim back to that continent, again arriving as shiny, glassy creatures the size of a match. Those whose parents swam from America go westward.

Eels also breed and hatch in the eastern Indian Ocean and the western and southern Pacific. They, too, migrate from the ocean to fresh water streams of Africa and Asia and return again.

The eel's migration is one, but merely one, of the many complex and amazing provisions which God has made so that his living ceratures may survive and carry on their species. Scientists have some very complicated and probably correct theories about the eel's travels. We won't go into them here. But the whole round trip, made only once through trackless ocean depths, covering a total of eight years, is even more amazing than the flight of migratory birds. At least the birds can see where they're going. The eels cannot.

Now some people might accept the eel's journey as a very dull, routine, and not exciting trip. But when I think about it I cannot help being overwhelmed once more by God's wonderful creation.

One man, the Danish scientist Johannes Schmidt, devoted decades of study to the eel. Are his theories on the eel's travels correct? We don't know. Perhaps your generation will solve the matter.

Other sea creatures make similar migrations but we won't describe them here. But whatever they are, God is back of every animal's every move. It is he that is their guide.

And so he guides us through the journey of life, a journey we make only once. But if we follow his lead we will arrive safely at our heavenly home, not to die, like the eel, but to live with him forever and ever.

# the miracles of Jesus

In that hour he cured many of diseases and plagues and
evil spirits, and on many that were blind he bestowed sight.
—Luke 7:21

How did Jesus heal the blind? How did he make
the cripple man walk or the deaf to hear? How did he
feed the multitude from five loaves of bread and two
fishes? How did he bring the dead man, Lazarus, back to
life? How did he perform all the other miracles or wonderful acts, which we read about in the four Gospels—
Matthew, Mark, Luke, and John?

In this modern age of science we believe that everything has a cause and effect. Each work of nature or of
man must have some reason or cause back of it.

When a jet airplane leaves the ground we know that
the cause of its flying is the force of the jet engines
which pushes it forward and up. But to peoples of another age a jet airplane or any airplane would have been
thought of as some god or angel or devil flying over.

Likewise, we know that an automobile is propelled by
an internal combustion engine which causes the wheels
to turn and the car to roll forward. Our ancestors living in
George Washington's time would have thought an automobile, without a horse out in front pulling it, a work
of magic.

And going not so far back in history, any doctor who
could prevent measles, pneumonia, smallpox, or

diphtheria might truly have been regarded as some kind of magician or wonder worker.

We could go on all day listing commonplace acts of this modern scientific age which in Jesus' time would have been thought incredible acts.

The acts which he did that his friends could not understand are called miracles. As yet we do not understand how he did them, either. We don't have enough description of what went on at some of the miracle scenes to give any final explanation.

But this much we do know. He was far superior in his power to do great things than were others living at the time, just as we are superior in some ways to our grandfathers. We know more than they knew. Jesus knew more than anybody of his time, and probably far more than many of our most learned men know today.

As the divine Son of God he had vast powers to read the human mind, to predict coming events, to give confidence and faith to those needing them, to perform acts which even today are regarded as miracles.

Years ago I did not believe that he performed these miracles. Because I could not understand I could not believe. But now I know that I understand so very few of the commonplace miracles such as electricity, light, digestion of food, human thought and memory. I do not understand them, I merely accept and use them.

So we accept the marvelous acts of Jesus as being done by one who has far greater understanding than we. And perhaps someday God will reveal to us how Jesus performed them.

Great though his deeds were Jesus never regarded

them as his greatest work. To make men love one another, to erase hatred, to kindle love, to make us want forgiveness for our sins, to cause us to love God—these were the greatest miracles he performed.

And they are the ones most needed today. Don't you agree?

# *some things science cannot do*

A man's life does not consist in the abundance of his possessions.—Luke 12:15

Have you ever tried to measure a heartache or weigh a laugh? Have you ever tried to put a disappointment in a test tube or observe your fears under a microscope? Have you ever tried to manufacture happiness? Can love be bought in a can or frozen in a package or stored in a refrigerator?

The answer to all these is no. And it will always be no. Why? Because there are some things science, however powerful, simply cannot do.

We live in a scientific age. And the future will be much more controlled by scientific discoveries than now. Someday men will learn how to conquer all diseases. There will be no more cancer or heart disease or polio or measles or tuberculosis or muscular dystrophy. There will be no more famine. Men everywhere will have enough to eat.

It is even possible, and this is a much harder thing to achieve, that there will be no more wars.

But if we make life a heaven on earth through science, we can still be miserable, mean, unhappy, and outright dangerous. For human beings are not like animals, satisfied with a full stomach and a warm place to sleep. We have just begun when we've gotten those things. We require satisfactions for the mind and soul.

And no matter how happily situated we are there is still something about the human being which makes him do wrong even though there is no excuse for it. The story of Adam and Eve disobeying God and risking expulsion from their perfect home, the Garden of Eden, illustrates how man will go against his own welfare.

Science can do no more than provide us with conditions for a good, happy life. And when these conditions are too perfect we can do bad things simply out of boredom.

Science cannot tell us right from wrong—and how badly we need to know many times. But no instrument, microscope, or testing machine can do what the voice of conscience can—tell us when we are wrong or right.

Science cannot give us ideals for which to live and die. And man cannot live without ideals, however hard he might try. He needs something to live for and look up to.

Science cannot make us love one another more, and that's what the world needs most today. It cannot make us forgiving and kind. It cannot keep us from saying biting words, nor can it erase biting words already spoken. It cannot make us want to sacrifice our welfare or give our money to those in need. In fact, the more we have the more selfish we are apt to become.

Jesus had everything, yet had nothing. He had no home, no money, no earthly power. Yet today he is the most powerful person on earth. He was rich in spiritual qualities, none of which came through science.

Have you ever tried buying friendship or analyzing it in a laboratory? It can't be done. But by the age-long process of being a true friend you will have true friends.

We like to look outside ourselves for answers to the hardest problems of life. So we think science and what it can provide us will bring happiness. This is not so at all.

Some things science cannot and never will be able to do. Read the story of the foolish rich man in Luke 12:13-21. It still applies today.

# *man's dependence on God's nature*

God said to them, "Be fruitful and multiply, and fill the earth and subdue it; and have dominion over the fish of the sea and over the birds of the air and over every living thing that moves over the earth."—Gen. 1:28

Because most Americans live in the city today, we seldom think of how much we are dependent on nature. We buy milk from a coin dispenser, get water from a faucet, food from the supermarket, and medicine from the nearby drugstore. We think that by making more machines and factories we can live comfortably by our own wits.

But without the cooperation of nature we couldn't live long. And if we upset the delicate balances which nature, or God, has set up we endanger our very existence.

All our foods come from fields and farms. They depend largely on rain and snow for water. No rain—no crops or pasture. Hence, no milk, no bread, no oranges. If drouth continues long enough, the reservoirs holding our city water supply dry up. There is no water from the faucet, no water in farm wells. Precious water is brought in and rationed. Already around New York City a water famine looms—too many people, too much sewerage, too little fresh water. Nature strikes back at our misuse of her.

How important is the bee to men? If all bees suddenly died, it is estimated that 100,000 species, or kinds, of plants would disappear from the earth, including many essential to men's food production.

How important are microbes to us? We can't see them but we can use them. Most of our lifesaving wonder drugs are microbes which eat other microbes when injected inside our bodies.

Suppose we had to get rid of all our immense city sewer waste by dumping it in nearby streams. What a horrible smell our land would soon have! Fortunately friendly microbes, if given a chance under proper conditions in modern sewerage disposal plants, eat our garbage

45

and give us a useful fertilizer as a by-product. Only when we work with nature instead of against her can man survive.

How important are trees to men's survival? Perhaps we could live without them, but it would be a poorer life indeed. Our forests provide watersheds which hold our fresh, clear drinking water; they prevent lands from eroding and washing into the sea; they give us a place to relax on vacation. Where men have foolishly destroyed timber covers, we have paid a heavy price.

Grass is our most important single plant. Most of men's farm animals' food is grass in some form—either ordinary pasture grass or such members of the grass family as wheat, oats, corn, rye, or barley. We eat seeds of these grasses in various forms as well as products from sugarcane, a well-known member of the grass family. And we mustn't fail to mention bamboo, a large, woody grass, which is very important to men in the tropics.

Fish not only provide food, but recreation as well. Again, they're God created, not manmade.

In the city pigeons, starlings, and sparrows are the most evident of all birds. But if all birds in the world were destroyed, insects would make life impossible for man in less than seven years. Men didn't make birds. God did. But we can destroy them.

If you ever have an opportunity visit a farm or better still, live there for a while. You'll see how dependent we are on nature.

We must respect the laws of nature, not upset them. Every living thing has a God-given purpose, was put

46

here for a reason. Use nature properly and she is our servant. Misuse her and she punishes us.

# *steering by the stars*

And lo, the star which they [the wise men] had seen in the East went before them, till it came to rest over the place where the child was. When they saw the star, they rejoiced exceedingly with great joy.—Matt. 2:9-10

When men are on long journeys and have no nearby landmarks to set their courses by, what do they use for guideposts? *Stars!*

Men have done this for many thousands of years. Ancient travelers over the eastern deserts, riding their camels by night to escape the terrible heat of the day, kept their direction by watching the stars above.

Hundreds of years ago, without compass or instrument of any kind, the South Pacific islanders sailed thousands of miles across the trackless ocean with the stars by night and the sun by day as their main sources of direction. Sailors of all nations have done the same.

And now the great atomic submarines travel under the ice pack of the Arctic Ocean, guided by unseen stars. These submarines are equipped with a marvelous instrument which takes a picture of the starry heavens before submerging beneath the ice, then "remembers" the

47

stars' locations as the vessel cruises thousands of miles without seeing the stars at all.

Sailors and travelers, and very soon the men who man the space ships will steer by the stars. Why? Because they don't change. They are always in one place, always reliable, always dependable.

For a short journey, small landmarks are fine. But for the distant trip, when no landmarks are around, as on the desert, on the ocean, under Arctic ice, out in the vast outer space, men want something dependable to steer by, something high, something never failing—stars.

You and I, all of us, are on a long trip—the journey of life. We want some inner guide signals which are the same all the way. And God, who waits at the end of the road, has provided such guide signals.

What are they? They are his laws, his rules, his teachings, especially those given by his Special Son, Jesus Christ. They are not manmade but God-made. They never change. They are always reliable.

God's commands to us are useful and reliable anytime, anyplace, any age. We can use them whether we are ten years old or fifty, or a hundred. And if we fail to use them we get off the true road of life. We get lost.

Sometimes, like the stars, God's ways for us are hard to see or remember. But if we remember them the best we can and learn them by heart they remain in our minds always.

On a long journey men set their courses by the stars, whether in submarine, outrigger canoes, sailing ships, airplanes, or space ships.

On the long journey of life, let us guide our lives by

God's wishes and commands for us, which are just as real and reliable as the stars in the heavens which our Heavenly Father also made.

## *some questions computers can't answer*

And a ruler asked him, "Good Teacher, what shall I do to inherit eternal life?"—Luke 18:18

How long will it take a certain type missile weighing a certain amount and powered a certain way to reach the moon if fired on such and such a morning at five o'clock from Cape Kennedy, Florida? Feed the parts of this problem into a giant electronic brain and you can get the answer.

How many baby girls will be born in California next October? Almost to a baby a computer will tell you. The same goes for such questions as: How many gallons of jet fuel will a certain type jet liner need to fly from New York to Los Angeles at five hundred miles an hour, thirty thousand feet high, against a twenty mile headwind? What should be the trajectory, or path, of a rocket ship flying from Chicago to Buenos Aires?

But give even the largest electronic computer a simple question like this: Does John love Mary? Will Albert

49

propose to Susan? Should I apologize to my mother for being cross? Should Pamela or Karen wash the dishes tonight? Should Johnny continue snitching candy in the drugstore because of the thrill or stop now? Should seventeen-year-old Mike go out drinking with his friends or go home early? Should I go to church next Sunday or watch the late, late movie Saturday night and sleep all Sunday morning? How can I prepare my soul for the next world?

Try getting answers for these questions from a computer, if you can. Even the most brilliant scientist wouldn't know what to put on the electronic tape that goes into the machine.

No computer has been invented, or ever will be, which will give us answers to these questions.

They are questions dealing with right and wrong, conduct and attitudes toward other people, duty, honor, our dealings with God, prayer, mercy, forgiveness, love, and courage.

They are the old, old questions. And they need old, old answers—not answers from a machine, but answers from the hearts; answers from the Bible, that great answer Book for the hard questions; answers from the church, where God's way is taught; answers from prayer, from asking God to show us the right way; answers which come from patiently waiting for God to show us. These are the hard answers, which come not with the pushing of a button and the feeding of a punched tape.

As long as we have such questions we will need the Bible, the church, and Sunday school. We will need

Christian people to help provide the answers. No machine can or will.

Is it right or wrong for me to do this or that? Sometimes a kindly, Christian friend can help decide, along with prayer and conscience.

Should a boy enter a certain field of work to make a lot of money or another, which he likes best, to give the greatest service to mankind? No machine can give the right answer or make him happy if he decides wrongly.

We need more and more to study God's word, to pray ceaselessly, to keep our conscience clean, to seek continually God's will. And even so, the hardest questions can only be answered in the human heart.

# *evolution—God's way of improving his creatures*

So God created man in his own image.—Gen. 1:27

Did man descend from monkeys? Did our ancestors swing from trees by their tails like Tarzan's friends still do? Are those really our cousins we see eating peanuts in the zoo?

These are terribly puzzling questions. So puzzling that many Christian young people simply quit thinking about them for fear they will arrive at the wrong answer—one which will destroy either their faith in God or their knowledge of science.

A part of the problem is the result of a misunderstanding. About one hundred years ago, in 1859, a very learned Englishman, Charles Darwin, published a book named *On the Origin of Species*. In it he showed how different animals have changed through the ages. Anyone who takes the time to read this book will know that Darwin never claimed we are descended from the monkey. This is only the mistaken idea of some people who really don't know what he said.

The process of change in plants and animals through the generations is called evolution. Evolution is going on all the time. Most of our farm animals and pets are good examples of evolution. Our dairy cows have been bred from runty, wild animals giving little milk to quiet, gentle beasts giving gallons a day. Our dogs and cats, especially dogs, are carefully bred to bring out certain qualities. This is evolution, though manmade and controlled.

We do the same with our crops—carefully developing through various complicated means a variety of corn, tomato, watermelon, or wheat which will yield a maximum harvest in a certain growing spot.

Perhaps the best single example of modern evolution is the turkey, which we have changed from a wild, tough, wiry bird to a small one with mostly white meat.

Evolution, then, means change—change of height, weight, appearance, strength, muscle, color, and other physical qualities.

Man has and man is changing all the time. In fact,

even today there are many kinds of men, judged by physical appearance. For example, there is the short, black, primitive pigmy of Africa, no bigger than an American sixth grader. There are four major races, each with skins of different color and even different kinds of hair.

American people are changing; since 1918 they have grown an inch taller and ten pounds heavier—a remarkably fast change, due mostly to better food and medicines. We are also living much longer.

Therefore, it does not bother me to think that my great-great-grandfather about a million years ago was hairy, used a club to kill bears and spank children, and even may have had a tail. He was still a man. Being a man with a soul, a mind, a sense of beauty, a feeling for God did not depend on outward physical qualities then any more than now. A white man, red man, black man, yellow man, or pigmy all can worship the one and same God.

Just as astounding is the way a Stone Age child from wildest New Guinea, whose favorite sport is head hunting, can be put in an American school, taught English, and graduate from our best college with honors the same as you and me. Apparently Stone Age people are as smart as we. Our missionaries have done exactly this—taken youths from Stone Age tribes and given them the highest college education.

Somewhere in the long distant past God created man in his own image—giving him a mind, a soul, a conscience, curiosity, and a sense of something beyond this physical world. Did he do it when man still lived by eating grubs, raw fish, and insects? I do not know. But he did do it. He created a new and different creature —man. Since we can't find a mind and soul in these most ancient skeletons scientists are digging up, it is possible we shall never know just when true man began. But true man began with God's act—just as the Bible says.

I am not afraid of evolution. To me it proves just how patient, wise, and wonderful God is.

# the good earth

And God said, "Let the earth put forth vegetation, plants yielding seed, and fruit trees bearing fruit which is their seed, each according to its kind, upon the earth." And it was so.—Gen. 1:11

In my hands I have some of the most ordinary, yet precious stuff in the world—dirt, just dirt. It is much like any found anywhere: black, rich, and capable of sprouting and growing most any seed you might plant in it—corn, wheat, watermelon, weeds, flowers, or pumpkins.

Why is something so commonplace so precious? Well, to tell the truth, dirt like this is rarer than you might think. Three fourths of the earth is covered with ocean water not by land. Of the land areas much is covered by ice, rocky mountains, sandy dry deserts, and frozen areas unusable by man. But only a tiny fraction of our globe is covered by black, rich earth actually usable for growing crops or furnishing grass for our farm animals and wild life.

It took about five billion years for God to produce this black fertile soil. First, there was a fiery ball, then a globe of rocks broken by oceans and spewing forth volcanic rock and ash. Many millions of years passed before any soil, such as we know it, was made from broken and ground-up rock. All the soils we know were once rock, whether they are clay, sand, loam, gravel, or whatever kind.

These rocks have been ground, pulverized, powdered, carried by streams, buried under oceans, brought again to the surface, utilized by plants and animals innumerable times throughout the ages until we now have this extremely precious few inches of topsoil which grows practically all we eat and wear. Destroy this thin layer of soil and you destroy man's ability to live at all.

When the white man arrived in America he found the richest continent in the world with deep, deep, black, rich soil in forest and plain. Foolishly he cut down the trees, plowed unwisely, broke up the prairies where he shouldn't have, and we have lost forever through erosion countless billions of tons of rich soil it took God many ages to create. Fortunately we are realizing our mistake and, through soil saving or soil conservation, are trying now to preserve our land from more waste.

In addition to the actual grains of soil in my hand there are multitudes of invisible little plants and animals, unseen to the naked eye but visible under a microscope. In a spoonful of such soil there may be dozens of kinds of such "germs," each with millions of their own kind. They enrich and make more usable the soil, decomposing last year's plant life, and doing a hundred other useful tasks to make this soil richer. This soil contains a regular universe of plant and animal life, much of it very valuable. Many of our modern wonder drugs come from this tiny life under our feet.

In America we have had so much rich soil that we are careless about it. Slowly we are learning, as other nations learned long ago, that God created just so much and when that's gone, it's gone for good.

Just dirt under your feet? No, the good, good earth, one of God's most marvelous creations.

# *metamorphosis*

And when I go and prepare a place for you, I will come again and take you to myself, that where I am you may be also.—John 14:3

Cats really don't have nine lives but insects do have four. At least they have four stages of the same life so that you could almost say that they're having four different lives in succession.

Here's the life cycle of most insects. First, the mother

56

insect lays the egg. This is the first stage and the insect is a helpless, soft little dot, often of a beautiful color.

The next stage is the *larva*. Another name for this stage is the caterpillar which we see in so many sizes, colors, and places. Many crop enemies are insects in this second stage. We see them gnawing away happily on tomato, potato, and other garden plants. The tent caterpillar even builds himself a silky home in the trees, eating the tree leaves meanwhile.

Then the insect spins himself a cocoon, slowly weaving a waterproof, weatherproof coat over his body and hitching this self-made home securely onto tree bark, under a leaf, or in some other protected place. Inside, while winter winds blow, the larva or caterpillar changes to the *pupa* with a shell which slowly hardens and assumes the shape of the full grown insect, complete with wings, legs, and head.

Spring comes, and there emerges from the silky cocoon the adult insect itself, complete in every detail. It gnaws out of its comfortable home, stretches its legs and wings, and away it flys.

Insects vary quite widely in the time and process of change, but they all have to pass through these stages in one way or another. That's part of being an insect. Some remain as a larva for several years underground. One, the seventeen-year locust or cicada, remains in the ground for seventeen years only to emerge and enjoy a few weeks of adult locusthood, lay its eggs, then die.

This change of life for insects is called *metamorphosis*. We human beings go through life stages, too, only we just get bigger instead of changing form like the insect. Before we are born we change shape rapidly. Then we are babies, next children, next youth, then young married people, middle-aged folks, then if we are lucky we live to be elderly people.

Each change of life is new to us. Some of us are afraid of the next step. For instance, the first few days in school may have been a dreadful adventure for some of us until we learned to like school. Many children move from one school or home to another and most make new friends, meet new teachers, adjust to new neighborhoods. Frequently such moves take great courage for boys and girls.

The process of growing up means new challenges, new tasks, and new opportunities. Years ago I liked school so much I dreaded to think of graduating. Yet, I have never regretted either the many years I spent in school or the fact that I no longer attend. The study and preparation of school has made my adult years more pleasant. Each stage of life is a preparation for another.

Perhaps if we human beings, and insects also, had the choice of remaining in one stage of life forever we would do it *if* the stage we were in were pleasant enough. But God has provided otherwise. And he knows best.

I have before me butterfly specimens in four stages— egg, caterpillar, pupa, and beautiful butterfly. Wouldn't it be a tragedy if this insect had the choice and power of remaining an egg, caterpillar, or pupa instead of becoming this glorious yellow creature, the mature butterfly?

The change we human beings dread most of all is

changing from this life to the next. This change we call *death*. Unlike the dying insect, dying human beings have the promise of another life beyond this. And the shift from our present human form to our heavenly life is even more glorious than the change of the caterpillar to beautiful butterfly. Nothing compares to it.

The great good news of the Easter Resurrection story of Christ is the promise of a new, better, more wonderful life for us beyond death.

We cannot prevent death any more than the insect pupa can prevent itself from becoming a butterfly. But we can so live here, so love God, so follow Christ that we shall be ready to live in that unknown but promised time and place which Jesus told us he was preparing for us.

In all four Gospels and in the letters of Paul we have promise after promise of our final metamorphosis. And what a glorious change it will be.

We are born, grow up, and die. This is God's plan for us. With his help we can make each stage of this life and the next a glorious one. And Jesus is waiting for us in that wonderful place beyond death.

# is man important in the universe?

When I look at thy heavens, the work of thy fingers,
   the moon and the stars which thou hast established;
what is man that thou art mindful of him,
   and the son of man that thou dost care for him?
Yet thou hast made him little less than God,
   and dost crown him with glory and honor.—Ps. 8:3-5

Frequently when reading science books we run across such thoughts as these: "On a tiny speck of dust [earth] revolving about an average size sun among billions of other similar suns, some bigger, in the Milky Way, which is only one of billions of galaxies in the Universe, lives an insignificant creature walking upright, living only a few years before death snuffs him out. This is man."

Now all this is perfectly true, and more. We are so tiny compared to our earth, our sun, our solar system, our Milky Way galaxy, and the universe that it is impossible to draw a picture on the biggest sheet of paper, including both our solar system and man. The dot representing man would be so small no microscope could possibly find it.

Some science writer has said that all the people in the world could be placed in a huge square box one-half mile long on each side. If this box were dropped into the Pacific Ocean, man would be done for.

Just how important is man? If he is so small, does he really count with God? And if so small, living such a short life here on earth, what's the use of the individual man and woman, boy and girl trying to live a good life, do noble deeds, or do anything except what pleases him or her at the moment? Does it really make sense to try when we amount to so little?

Well, strange as it may seem, we *do* count. God *does* care for us. We are worth something. A good life *is* worth trying.

Let's imagine for a moment that your father is the richest man in the world. In fact, he owns the world—all the oil wells, all the gold, silver, diamonds, railroads, ships, banks, stores, and the rest.

Then one day you were born—a mere baby, tiny, helpless, depending on your parents for everything, unable to repay them for their love and care. Let us go farther and imagine that you were born with some physical defect, as some children are, so that you could never care for yourself.

Now, which would your father, if he were a good father, love the most—you or all his oil wells, gold, silver, diamonds, railroads, ships, banks, and stores? You know the answer—you would count most in his eyes. You would be worth more to him than all his riches.

Remember the old story of Midas, the greedy, gold-loving king, who turned his daughter into gold by his magic touch then realized that her life meant more to him than all his riches?

You and I mean more to God than all the physical universe—all the oceans, moons, stars, and galaxies. For we are his children.

We are not crawling specks of dust but immortal children of a loving Heavenly Father. How we live makes a

61

vast difference to him. So much so that he sent his Son, Jesus Christ, to teach us. Doesn't this show something of how important we are to God?

How we live does make a difference. It makes a difference to us. It makes a difference to friends and family. Our example may inspire them. And finally, the kind of soul we have here on earth, we take with us. Forever and forever we will live, not just a few years.

A speck of dust or an immortal child, loved by God? Which do you think makes the most sense?

# greater miracles than Jesus'?

Truly, truly, I say to you, he who believes in me will also do the works that I do; and greater works than these will he do, because I go to the Father.—John 14:12

How amazing were the miracles of Jesus when he performed them in Galilee! Healing the blind, curing the epileptic, opening the ears of the deaf, turning water into wine, walking on the water, feeding the five thousand with a few loaves of bread and fishes, making the paralyzed walk, the dead to live again, the feverish mother-in-law of Peter to get up instantly cured, and all the other hard-to-believe miracles.

No wonder the crowds followed him. Such a miracle worker would attract crowds today, too, especially if he could cure people of their painful diseases. If you had been sick for years, wouldn't you make every effort to see such a man?

And so the crowds followed Jesus until he asked them to take part in the greatest miracle of all—the change of a human heart when given entirely to him. Then the crowds fell away at such a demand and only a few disciples remained.

Yesterday, while sitting outside, I saw the white vapor trail of a jet plane slowly cross the sky, many miles high, too high for the plane itself to be seen. Just another jet plane. If it had appeared over Jerusalem when Jesus lived, the crowds would have shouted: "A visitor from heaven! What can this mean?" But we moderns hardly raise our eyes when a jet plane passes overhead.

Jesus knew that man, with his God-given mind, would accomplish miracles which would make his seem small. In his last talk with his disciples recorded in John 14 he predicted, "Greater works than these will he do." Already his prophecy has come true.

Jesus healed paralyzed people one at a time. Through the Salk vaccine we can prevent millions of people from being paralyzed. Which is a greater miracle?

He fed the five thousand. Today, through modern agriculture, we raise fantastic crops and animals. In America we even have a food surplus.

We not only circle the earth in space ships, we now plan trips to the moon, Mars, Venus, and beyond. Already true space ships are being planned and built. Jesus performed no such miracles except when he ascended to God through a cloud after his Resurrection.

Is Jesus jealous that we perform such miracles? Not

at all. His prediction is coming true. We are using our minds for the benefit of mankind.

Now Jonas Salk, the great polio scientist, predicts that within a short time we will have a single vaccine which will give us immunity to perhaps twenty diseases at once! "Greater works" indeed!

God wants us to learn more and more of his world.

But still the greatest miracle of all is the hardest. And no medical doctor can inject it with a cure-all disease preventative. Nor can it be achieved by sending men to the moon or by splitting the atom.

The greatest miracle occurs inside us, when we turn from our hateful, selfish, cruel ways and become forgiving, loving, tenderhearted, and humble. This greatest miracle can only happen when we let it. God performs it when he changes our hearts at our request. And unless this miracle happens, scientific miracles only produce more misery for mankind.

Yes, the greatest miracle of all happens now and forever will happen within the human heart.

## why not just one color?

O Lord, how manifold are thy works!
In wisdom hast thou made them all.—Ps. 104:24

Why so many colors? Why not just one single color, such as red, gray, green, or blue? Why did God bother to create the hundreds of shades of colors we see on every hand?

Certain people are color blind. They see only black, gray and white. So, it is said, does a dog. He never sees a sunset. He never sees the green leaves, the blue sky, or the red flowers. They all appear in shades of gray.

The study of colors is very important as it applies to printing, cloth making and dying, painting, or the study of nature.

Certain colors, called primary colors, make up white or white light. White sunshine can be divided by the glass prism into red, orange, yellow, green, blue, indigo, and violet, in that order. A disk divided like a pie into sections of these same colors, in the proportion in which they appear in the spectrum, and whirled rapidly appears white.

Colors make our world beautiful to see.

And sounds make it wonderful to hear! Imagine being deprived of hearing beautiful music, bird's singing, a child laughing, or the thousand and one other sounds which come to our mysteriously made ear, sounds which range from a few vibrations per second to thousands.

But why not just one sound? Why did God make so many?

And tastes! Why not just one taste, such as bitter, sweet, sour? Instead, we have hundreds: chocolate, vanilla, strawberry, tomato, watermelon, and hundreds of others. Suppose you had to eat all your foods without ever tasting them. Some people do—those whose taste is gone.

And why so many delightful smells? Why not just

one smell for everything? Instead, God has given us thousands. And nothing brings back memories of years gone by more vividly than an odor. Just a whiff and our mind goes back so quickly! I am glad that God gave us so many odors. The few unpleasant ones we endure only make the rest all the better.

And what about the various kinds of feelings? Ah, God has made a good world here, too: the feel of clean sheets, the feel of swimming in cool water after a hot day, the feel of resting when exhausted, the sensation of ice skating outside on a clear, crisp night. All these feelings and sensations, and thousands more!

God gave us variety in our senses. Not just one color, sound, taste, smell, or sensation. He gave us thousands and thousands of combinations.

Some people live merely to enjoy their senses. Any good thing God has given us can be abused and overdone.

But God gave us these senses for protection and enjoyment. To fail to see him in the sights, sounds, tastes, odors, and feelings around us is to be blind indeed. To never lift one's eye to the sunrise and sunset is to miss God in the sky. To fail to hear him in the myriad sounds around is to miss him through the ear. To fail to appreciate him in the many tastes and odors is to ignore that it is he who gave us these tastes and odors and the abilities to know them.

Helen Keller, one of the world's greatest women, blind, deaf, and dumb, gives us this advice in her autobiography, entitled *The Story of My Life:*

I who am blind can give one hint to those who see—one admonition to those who would make full use of the gift of sight: Use your eyes as if tomorrow you would be stricken blind. And the same method can be applied to the other senses. Hear the music of voices, the song of a bird, the mighty strains of an orchestra, as if you would be stricken deaf tomorrow. Touch each object you want to touch as if tomorrow your tactile sense would fail. Smell the perfume of flowers, taste with relish each morsel, as if tomorrow you would never smell and taste again. Make the most of every sense: glory in all the facets of pleasure and beauty which the world reveals to you through the several means of contact which nature provides. But of all the senses, sight must be the most delightful.

## *our wonderful oceans*

The sea is his, for he made it.—Ps. 95:5

Although we live on land, seven tenths of the world's surface is covered by water—the oceans. Forever moving, forever tossing restlessly, each connected by endless plains of water, the oceans of the world are so vast and full of amazing wonders that we could study them for a lifetime and know just a tiny bit about them.

No one can stand on the seashore without wondering how large the ocean is. Even a large steamer may travel many days without sighting another ship. Men in lifeboats have floated for weeks without being seen. The ocean is very large and very lonely.

The ocean has many moods and colors—stormy, gay, placid, blue, green, gray, ugly, angry, smiling, and outright dangerous. Its friendly rolling swells can build up into towering fifty-foot waves powerful enough to sink or damage our largest ships.

The five largest oceans in order of size are: the Pacific, which is twenty-one times larger than the United States in area; the Atlantic, the Indian, the Antarctic, and the Arctic. The Pacific Ocean alone occupies approximately one third of the entire surface of our earth.

Ocean water is rich in chemicals. One cubic yard—that is, a tank of sea water three feet high, three feet wide, and three feet deep—contains the following: forty-six pounds of table salt, two pounds of magnesium, almost a pound of calcium, and over a pound of sulfur. All the oceans together contain enough gold to give every person in the world about nine pounds of this precious yellow metal.

The average depth of our oceans is two and one-third miles. If Mt. Everest were sunk in its deepest part more than a mile of water would cover its peak.

Earth's largest animal, the whale, swims in the ocean, though it is a mammal, not a fish.

If all the land in the world were leveled flat, over a mile and half of ocean water would cover the entire globe. Although water cannot be compressed, or made smaller by pressure, as air can be, its weight adds up when water is piled on water. In the deepest part of the sea over twelve thousand pounds per square inch of weight press on the ocean floor, so great is the weight of the water above.

Most of our weather comes from the ocean. Since water heats or cools slowly compared with air, our oceans provide warm air in winter and cool air in summer for our great land area. Also the mighty ocean currents, more immense than a hundred Mississippis or Amazons, take cool or warm weather from one area to another. Western Europe is far to the north of the United States, yet its climate is similar because the Gulf Stream takes warm weather from our Gulf of Mexico.

In many ways the vastness, immensity, seemingly endless power of the ocean reminds us of God. God's love is endless, too. It has no beginning and no end, just like God himself. The ocean's breezes make life possible for us. God's love does also.

The ocean's riches provide us with life. All life originally came from ocean water. So, also, does all life come from God.

# *is God in outer space?*

If I ascend to heaven, thou art there!—Ps. 139:8

When John Glenn whirled around the earth on February 20, 1962, he was the first American to circle this globe in a spaceship. By the time you read this others will have done the same.

This raises a question: If and when men travel to the distant planets and stars, will God be there?

Many centuries ago men thought their god or idol was able to rule over just their own land or nation. In the ancient Hebrew nation the Israelites thought of their God, or Jehovah, as being supreme over just their land. Their neighboring nations thought the same. When men went from one land to another they might take a load of earth from their god's native place to their new residence so that the god would feel at home.

When Naaman, the mighty Syrian warrior, was healed of leprosy by the prophet Elisha (II Kings 5) he took two mules' load of earth from Elisha's property so that Elisha's God would feel at home back in Syria! Fantastic, but true. Little did the sincere, but mistaken, Naaman know that God is everywhere.

Somehow we earth inhabitants have assumed that God lives more on this earth with us than anywhere else. Like Naaman, we connect him with a certain place. How silly, when God created the most distant star millions of light years away as surely as he did the ground beneath your feet!

When our spaceships explore the tiny bit of space around us, we will hardly be going out of our own front yard, or beyond the next house. And God will be there. For he's been there all along.

They are his stars, his planets, his suns, his star systems, his galaxies, his space however thin it might be. They all operate by his laws, sustained by his love.

If our great-great-grandchildren discover distant human cousins on a distant planet, they too will be God's children, as much as you and I. Those future explorers might feel somewhat like Christopher Columbus felt when he discovered the America.

Wherever we go, whatever we do, God is there.

And he is there, too, in those places and times of loneliness, right here on earth, when we feel as much by ourselves, forgotten, and lonely as if we were deserted on a distant planet.

Is God in outer space? Is he in your church, your school, your city, our nation, in Europe, in Asia? He is in all these places at once.

When young Gherman Titov, Russian astronaut, circled the globe seventeen times in August, 1962, he looked in vain for God. Said he: "Some people say there is a God out there. But in my travels around the earth all day long I looked around and didn't see him. I saw no God or angels."

Though Mr. Titov may be a brilliant and a brave man, this was a childish statement, as we well know. The most important things in life are not necessarily visible things. No one has ever seen gravity, for that matter. But it took a powerful rocket to blast Mr. Titov out beyond gravity's mighty pull, just the same.

When our spacemen explore places not dreamed of by even Buck Rogers the same loving Heavenly Father who protects and saves us here will be waiting. He will be no closer or farther away than he is here. Which is to say—he is very close indeed!

71

# does God want new scientific discoveries?

*Thou hast given him dominion over the works of thy hands; thou hast put all things under his feet.—Ps. 8:6*

Does God want us to discover more, invent more, delve more into the mysteries of nature, which only open more mysterious mysteries and reveal more questions for us to ponder? Does he resent our finding out the hidden secrets of the universe? Is he jealous of our increasing knowledge? Will he punish us for using the brains he gave us for seeking out answers our minds seem to raise willy nilly whether we want to or not?

Some people fear that already we have discovered too much for our own good. And indeed there seems to be reason for this fear. How are we going to control our use of the atom and hydrogen bombs which science has invented? How can we stop the destruction of all mankind, perhaps of all animal life except that of the insects, by these terrible weapons?

But there is no stopping of our learning or none in sight. And would God want us to stop? Hardly. For does any good father want his children to stop learning? Surely God is concerned with our use of what we learn. He must want us to use our knowledge for helping not hurting ourselves and others. But are we to put a STOP sign on the road of science? Not when he has given us our marvelous minds to seek out knowledge.

72

Can men live in good health to the age of one hundred years? Or two hundred? Can science prolong our lives in good health this long?

Can sea water be converted into fresh water and transported to dry farm land inland cheaply enough to "make the desert blossom like the rose" as the Bible predicted?

Can mental illnesses be cured or prevented by vaccines? Can most of our present diseases such as cancer, tuberculosis, and birth defects be prevented or cured? Can vital parts of our bodies be transplanted, as bits of bone are today?

Can climate be controlled for man's benefit?

Can we discover the secret of food synthesis which occurs in green leaves and grass every day—the conversion of sunlight, oxygen, water, and carbon into usable foods?

Will we ever really contact other worlds in distant space or send expeditions there?

Yes, I believe God would be pleased if we could do all these things and more, provided, at the same time, we learned to take more seriously the wisdom and truth he gave us almost two thousand years ago when he sent Jesus Christ his Son here.

For it is in the soul and spirit that we find our hardest, most difficult area of achievement. Long after the first American has landed on the moon our most urgent problems will be right here on earth. Why can't we get along as neighbors? Why do we gossip about our friends? Why do nations go to war? Why are we greedy for more money than we need? Why are we selfish? Why do we betray our friends? Why must the Negroes take the low-

73

est paying jobs? Why won't we let Negroes live in certain places in our towns, with nobody selling them houses in those areas? How can we get husbands and wives, brothers and sisters, to treat one another as they should? Why don't we forgive those who have hurt us instead of hurting them back?

Yes, man should explore, invent, delve out. Only let him work also at the same time in applying the spiritual laws of God given by Jesus. Otherwise the scientific laws will surely destroy us.

# *what's inside the atom?*

O Lord, how manifold are thy works!
In wisdom hast thou made them all.—Ps. 104:24

Until just a few decades ago even the wisest men assumed that the atom was the smallest thing in existence and that it could not be changed.

Through modern scientific instruments we are finding that, instead of being a solid little item like a buckshot or mustard seed with no open places or changes inside, the inside of any atom, whether it be an atom of hydrogen, gold, silver, oxygen, or carbon, is a beehive of ceaseless activity, never still, forever changing, restless as restless can be.

Men used to wonder if there was such a thing as perpetual motion, that is, something which never stopped moving. Actually the entire universe is forever moving, and no part of it moves more ceaselessly or rapidly than the interior of the atom.

At the center of each atom is the heavy nucleus. Spinning around it at thousands of miles per hour are rings of electrons, with a certain number in each ring, ranging from just one electron in the case of hydrogen, the lightest gas, and running up into almost a hundred in the case of lead, gold, and heavier metals.

Though the atom is too small to be seen by the most powerful microscope, we know that if we could enlarge it we would find that these electrons are a vast distance from the nucleus, spinning forever. If the nucleus were as big as a baseball, the nearest electron would be many thousands of miles away. Yet all this motion is going on in a space smaller than we can imagine.

If the atom is in a gaseous or liquid state, such as air or water, it is moving about at a furious rate, bumping into other atoms at a terrible speed. If our ears were sensitive enough to hear these bumpings, we would be overwhelmed with sound—like millions of firecrackers going off every second, night and day.

Inside the nucleus, which formerly was thought to be a solid ball, are some thirty or more tiny particles, each forever moving restlessly at a rate of speed which would make us dizzy if we could see them in motion.

What holds all this together? Scientists wish they knew. What is the glue of the universe? What keeps our bodies, houses, pets, pencils, schoolhouses, friends, and families from flying apart into thin nothingness, with all this clatter and commotion going on in the smallest parts of us, the atom? We don't know.

But we do realize more than ever that the atom is in itself a small universe, or solar system, with a center like the sun and with electrons representing the planets, forever moving around the center. And behind it all is a God whose power and wisdom are great enough to keep each atom together.

# tree rings

But rejoice in so far as you share Christ's sufferings, that you may also rejoice and be glad when his glory is revealed. —I Pet. 4:13

I have a cross section of a tree, sawed straight across, which was taken from near the bottom of the trunk. So ordinary is this section that it's hardly worth taking a second look at it. We've all seen such sections or pictures of them.

But wait. Let's examine it. Perhaps there's a human interest story here. In the center are several rings widely spaced—that was when the tree was young and shooting up rapidly. Then, they seem to get thinner and thinner. That's true of most tree rings. But the tree was growing rapidly, just the same.

Here's a very, very thin ring near the middle. That

76

year, about thirty years ago, was very dry. So the tree grew very little. The next ring, representing the next year, was three times as wide, showing that much rain fell during the spring and summer.

Each ring has two parts, a soft and a hard part, with the hard part coming in the fall to cap off the year's growth.

Does the tree continue to grow inside? No, only the outer, outside edge grows, while the inner rings of previous years, once the tree's growing edge next to the bark, harden and become the body of the tree. This process occurs in the limbs as well as in the tree trunk itself.

Scientists once thought of tree rings as just an interesting, curious fact of nature. But now they study them seriously; for by observing very old redwood trees' rings, tree trunks taken from Indian adobe-house ruins in the Southwest, and from fossil trees, they discover what the weather was like a certain year several hundreds or even thousands of years ago. How much did it rain in A.D. 1049 in central California? Consult the tree rings of that year! The answer is there.

Or perhaps a forest fire raged in the same area in 1492, the year Columbus discovered America. The fire scar may be recorded in the wood.

The growth of human minds and souls may be somewhat like that of trees. There should always be a growing edge; a part of us which is absorbing new truth, new ideas; a fresh, vital, and changing part. Then that part of us which has come into our minds and hearts years ago stays there, like tree rings. Perhaps one year we grow

77

rapidly. The next, for some reason, we grow very little. Perhaps in one school year we studied little and learned little. The next year we worked hard and grew mentally at a great pace.

Some of us bear inner scars from being hurt. Instead of destroying us such incidents can make us stronger people.

Trees differ markedly in their rate of growth and, therefore, in the width of their rings. A fast-growing slash pine in southern Alabama may have half-inch rings. The slow-growing mahogany, oak, birch, cherry, or walnut may have thin rings. But the slow-growing trees, especially those which have grown in difficult places, have the most beautiful woods for furniture and lumber. So our own lives may be most beautiful when they have been tested through the years by hardships and adversities.

Our growing, outer edge is now. We have this year, this month, this week, this day, this minute to add to our lives. It will become a part of the record, like these tree rings. What is going into the growing edge of your life?

# where did matter come from?

In the beginning God created the heavens and the earth.
—Gen. 1:1

God . . . calls into existence the things that do not
exist.—Rom. 4:17

The paper and ink in this book, the air you breathe,
your body, the chair you sit in, the clothing you wear
are all made of what we call *matter*.

The universe is filled with two things—space and
matter. Space is just space—thin nothingness where, as
far as we know, there is nothing at all except perhaps
energy in some form. But wherever there is an atom or
collection of atoms we call this matter. Even in the
thinnest space between the stars, there is some matter.

Where did matter come from and what is becoming
of it? Where and how did it begin?

Matter is composed of elements, about one hundred
of them—solid ones, liquid ones, and gaseous ones. Iron,
lead, copper, mercury, hydrogen, chlorine, oxygen—
these are all elements.

Combine these elements in various ways and you
have chemicals, such as table salt from chlorine and
sodium or water from hydrogen and oxygen.

Combine them still further and you have plants and
animals, wood, clothing, and food. Of course this process
is more complicated. Everything we can see, touch, feel,
or taste is matter. And in the wonderful arrangement of
this matter which God has made and which we call our

79

bodies, our soul dwells while we are here on earth.

One theory scientists have says that all matter in the universe was once tightly packed together in a ball and that this ball exploded and the matter once in it is flying apart still, like an exploding bomb, in all directions at once, and the farther you get from the center of the explosion, the faster the matter is moving. This is called the *explosion theory of creation.*

Another theory is that of *continuous creation* of matter—that matter and energy are continually and forever being changed, one into the other, back and forth, the stars giving out energy which in the vast reaches of space gradually becomes matter again through a gradual collection process. When enough atoms have collected together they become stars again.

But neither of these ideas or others which we are constantly conceiving really explain how all this enormous amount of physical material in the universe ever got here in the first place. It is a tremendous question for man to even ask, much less answer. It is thrilling to realize that God has planted the question in our minds and that with the intelligence he gave us, we might even someday find the answer. Perhaps someone who is a boy or girl today will assist in the search.

Several lines in the Bible regarding creation are very interesting. In Ps. 33 we read, "By the word of the Lord the heavens were made," and "For he spoke, and it came to be." And in the book of Romans, fourth chapter, seventeenth verse we find these mysterious words about God—"And [he] calls into existence the things that do not exist."

Our Christian belief about matter is that God created it sometime, somehow, some place. About the details we are not sure. Perhaps man will never know them. But the search for the facts is exciting and worth the discovery just for the fun of finding out. God has made us curious about his mysterious and wonderful universe. So our minds won't rest until we've arrived at the best answer possible.

Where did matter come from? When? How? Is it all being destroyed, and will it gradually disappear into thin space? Will the universe run down and all the stars go out and become like cold, blackened cinders?

To answer these questions or find even a tiny, tiny part of the answer is a thrilling pursuit. When and if we get to the final answer we will find it to be a three-letter word—G–O–D.

Where did matter come from? Where is it going? That's for God to know and his human children to find out.

# *will science replace religion?*

Man shall not live by bread alone, but by every word that proceeds from the mouth of God.—Matt. 4:4

A world completely run by science? A world without churches? A nation without Sunday schools? A land

81

without the Bible? Will these ever come? Will men ever be so intelligent, reasonable, and orderly that they may discard Christian teachings and live happily by scientific principles? Some say "yes," that as we learn more about how to control nature we will gradually discard our religions as we have the oxcart and pony express.

But will it ever happen? I doubt it. For it is quite plain today that the more science brings us together the more we need the teachings of Jesus to get along peaceably.

When the Communists took over Russia after World War I they established a museum in Moscow to exhibit relics of the church to a new generation of children who were to live without the church. The museum was to depict the dark ages of men when religion was needed. Already this museum itself is out-of-date, for the church is still very much alive in Russia.

Voltaire, a brilliant Frenchman of two centuries ago, predicted that within a century the Bible would be forgotten, no longer read. Nietzsche, a brilliant German of a hundred years ago, predicted the same thing. How wrong both were!

Jean Jacques Rousseau, another well-known Frenchman, also predicted an early death for the Bible. Today his house is used as headquarters for the Swiss Bible Society. His ideas are the amusing relics of yesterday while the Bible is the living Light for today.

Perhaps for two main reasons man will always need the security, strength, and help which comes from our faith in God and Jesus Christ.

First of all, we are not just animals, with merely

animal needs for food, drink, and a place to sleep. We are immortal souls which need contact with God. Unless we have it our souls are unsatisfied. And science, with all its wonder and glory, cannot satisfy the needs of the soul.

Jesus, in rejecting the first of his three great temptations, said that man cannot live by bread alone. This is still true, and will ever be true. So, we cannot live by the miracles of modern science. We need God.

The other reason we have already mentioned. As life grows more complicated, with weapons of war more deadly, with rocket ships faster, with more and more people crowded close together, our need to get along peaceably together grows accordingly. In fact, this need becomes a necessity. Unless we can apply Christian teachings to war we will destroy one another. This is plain as the nose on your face.

Yes, we must admit that the church has failed many times, or its members certainly have. But man's need for God continues. And we have as yet found no substitute for the church and the Bible—nor are we likely to.

# God's saints of science

Not every one who says to me, "Lord, Lord," shall enter the kingdom of heaven, but he who does the will of my Father who is in heaven.—Matt. 7:21

A saint, as we think of one, is a person who is holy, godly, and who tries exceedingly hard to live just as God desires. Usually he is very active in the church.

We regard all the disciples, except Judas, as saints; also Stephen, the first Christian martyr; Paul, the first missionary and author of many letters in the New Testament; many of the early Christians immediately after Christ; and also church leaders of later centuries.

I would include Martin Luther, who helped purify the church; John Huss of Bohemia, who was burned alive; John Wycliffe and William Tyndale, who translated the Bible; David Livingstone, the great missionary to Africa; and also many other missionaries, such as Albert Schweitzer who is still living; and countless other individuals, who have tried to live holy lives. Nor should we forget women like Joan of Arc; Jane Addams, the American social worker; and Anne Sullivan, who taught Helen Keller to read, write, and speak.

Frankly I think it is a risky business to call some people saints even though they deserve the title, for we ignore so many others who also deserve it. So many of us have parents who are saints—if we think of somebody who is godly, holy, and who tries to do God's will at all times.

Since we're thinking of all kinds of saints, let's add another very important kind—the saints of science. Yes, the saints of science who with tremendously hard work, sacrifice, and frequently at the risk of torture, persecution, and death have revealed to mankind wonderful and useful truths about God's universe.

I am thinking of Galileo, who proved that the earth goes round the sun, not the sun around it; or of Isaac Newton, the kindly English genius of three centuries ago, the greatest scientist of all time. He wrote about his theories of light and color, the laws of gravitation, and invented calculus. And I am thinking of the great French Louis Pasteur, who proved that tiny germs cause disease. What abuse he suffered for daring to say such an unheard of thing, just a century ago, and how much we all owe to this patient, long-suffering man!

I would include Lister, Koch, Semmelweis—all great in medical history. In our own time I would include Jonas Salk, who with his microscope and horn-rimmed glasses so little resembles our idea of Paul or Peter. Yet, how much will his vaccine for polio benefit God's children!

Perhaps you can name many others whose daring, genius, and hard work have brought new and useful discoveries to man. Each in his own way, a saint of science, bringing more knowledge of God's universe to us.

The title to an old Negro spiritual goes like this: "When the Saints Go Marching In."

Well, if and when all of God's saints go marching in I am sure of this: Marching in with Peter, Paul, Joan of Arc, Martin Luther, John Wesley, and John Huss will be

85

saints of science, each of whom opened up another window of God's truth.

# *the backbone of a jellyfish*

Fear not, for I am with you,
be not dismayed, for I am your God;
I will strengthen you, I will help you,
I will uphold you with my victorious
right hand.—Isa. 41:10

Did you ever hear the expression, "He doesn't have the backbone of a jellyfish"? It's not a compliment, by any means. The person so described simply has no power to make his own decisions and stand by them.

All animals are classified as either vertebrates or invertebrates. The former have a backbone, the latter do not. Vertebrate animals have bones which extend through the body giving it form, strength, and protection.

Vertebrate animals often have a hollow-bone structure called the skull which protects the delicate and invaluable brain, which in turn directs the whole body. The spinal column is a series of bones running from the skull down the back. Through it runs the signal system of the body, the spinal cord, which is a collection of nerves carrying messages back and forth to the brain. Branching out from the spinal column are the legs, arms, and ribs which give strength and power to vertebrates.

A jellyfish is an extreme example of the invertebrate. When a wave washes him high up on the ocean beach he has no power to return to the water. Within an hour or so under the sun he's evaporated like so much water, which he mostly is.

Bones reinforce our bodies, giving them the ability to stand, sit, walk, or run. They are our framework. The 206 bones of the human body determine our shape. Without them the muscles and vital organs would collapse.

Our characters and souls need a backbone and skeleton too. We all need a few principles, ideas, and ideals which are so strong, solid, and dependable that our lives can have form, strength, power, and purpose. A life built without strong central convictions is like a body without a framework—in other words, like a jellyfish.

Our Puritan forefathers had strong moral backbones. They believed strongly in God's will for them and in the right of individuals to seek God in the Bible in his own way.

Our American government's skeleton is the Declaration of Independence and the Constitution of the United States and its amendments.

Religious beliefs, high ideals, Christian principles—these have no weight or color, nor can they be photographed by X ray as can our skeleton. But if we possess them strongly enough they can shape our lives and others' lives. Our nation is built on the religious convictions of individual men and women—people who have backbone.

When the chief founder of the Protestant faith, Martin Luther, was told he must take back the religious beliefs

87

he had written or face a horrible death, he spoke boldly: "Here I stand. I can do no other!" He wouldn't take back a word. That required backbone.

Backbone, too, is required when a boy or girl refuses to lower moral standards to please the crowd. Again, backbone, backbone, backbone! A human character or a jellyfish? We can be either one.

Hold fast to your finest and best ideals. You know what they are. Strengthen them by use. Never let them go. Do you want to be strong inside or be like the jellyfish, which anybody can push around and which any wave may push this way or that?

Nobody wants to be a jellyfish, but many people are. Having a backbone requires considerable courage. But God will provide it if you ask him.

# the creation story

In the beginning God created the heavens and the earth. The earth was without form and void, and darkness was upon the face of the deep.—Gen. 1:1-2

No scientific problem puzzles thinking Christians in this scientific age more than how and when the world was created. Among the smartest scientists there are conflicting ideas about the earth's beginning. Was it a dust cloud which gradually came together into a solid? Was it flung out from the sun? These are two main ideas of its beginning.

How old is the earth? Estimates from three billion to ten billion are talked about. Is it as old as the universe?

How can the Bible story of creation in the book of Genesis mean anything today? So much is left out of the Genesis story. And how could God create the world in a mere six days? Why, that's hard to imagine!

First of all, the Bible is not a scientific textbook, written to explain the sciences. It is a book of religion, about God and man. And if the Bible writers had tried to base the Bible's truth on the science of their day this great Book would have been out-of-date long ago. How completely science has changed even in the past fifty years. Suppose the Bible were based on science of 1850. Already it would be unbelievable.

But, strange as it may seem, the story of Creation in Genesis, the order of God's creation of the earth fits in so closely with what scientists have discovered that it can hardly be accidental.

Examine the order of creation in the first chapter of Genesis, which means "the beginnings."

First the "earth was without form and void." So it was, scientists believe, whether as a hot molten mass or a dust cloud. "Darkness was upon the face of the deep." Yes, we think now there were dense vapor clouds thousands of feet thick covering the earth for many millions of years.

"And God said, 'Let there be light.'" Then, scientists think, the mists descended as rain with only occasional clouds left, as we have now.

"And God said, 'Let the waters under the heavens be gathered together into one place, and let the dry land appear.' " And so the continents arose, later to change their shapes continually, as they still are changing.

Then, on the remaining "days" of Creation God formed first vegetation; then the moon and stars; then animals which started life in the ocean, including "great sea monsters" whose fossils we have now discovered; then the land animals which we now know followed sea animals when the first fishes climbed out on shore pushing themselves along with their fins; and finally the crowning creation of all, man.

How did it happen that the ancient Bible writer's story fits so closely in with what geologists know today? Could it have been accidental? No, I cannot help but believe that in this all-important explanation of our world he was told by God what to write.

And the dignity of the story ranks so high above other ancient creation explanations! The old Japanese, Hindu, Greek, Roman, and Babylonian theories sound perfectly childish and ridiculous compared to the Bible story. Yet they were believed and written at much the same time as the Bible account.

Best of all, our Genesis story has a Great Being with a Purpose starting our earth. No freakish gods or animals are involved. Only a God who, in the beginning, created the heavens and the earth.

As you grow older and study the sciences, read now and then the first two chapters of Genesis.

Perhaps you will be puzzled about the six "days" in which God created the earth. But in God's time a day may be a thousand, million, or a billion years. The Bible says that with the Lord a thousand years are like a day and a day like a thousand years. A "day" in the creation process could be a long period of many years.

When one grows weary of reading immense books explaining how our earth began, how comforting and restful it is to read the masterpiece of masterpieces on this subject—right in the first chapter of Genesis. Be sure to read it at least once a year as you study your sciences in high school and college.

# science and the second commandment

You shall not make for yourself a graven image . . . you shall not bow down to them or serve them; for I the Lord your God am a jealous God.—Deut. 5:8-9

When we see in movies or TV pictures of ancient peoples bowing down and worshiping bronze or stone figures which they called "gods" we have a great feeling of pity. We say, "How silly to think that something man can make should be worshiped."

In some cases parents actually sacrificed their children to these pieces of statuary. In the Bible we read how even the Hebrew people, when they wandered from God's commandments, would worship these false gods and, like their pagan neighbors, sometimes give the lives of their beloved sons and daughters to please the idols. Again and again in the Old Testament we read of God's people disobeying him to bow down before these silly figures.

The second of the Ten Commandments deals with just this problem. Given to the children of Israel through their leader Moses, it was written to meet the very real evil or idol worship.

Looking down our noses at these ancestors of ours we say, "How stupid!"

But wait—don't we do pretty much the same thing when we put the things we make before the God who made us?

We can give so much of our time, attention, and money to literally serving the products of modern science and industry that they can become our idols as much as the ancient statues were to the Hebrews, Philistines, and Syrians.

To worship means to give honor, respect, and attention. Isn't this what we do for the possessions we think we must have but don't really need—bigger cars, finer clothing, and luxuries we don't have to have?

Through the discoveries of science man now can own and use fantastic creations. They can become his idol— getting his honor, respect, attention, and reverence much more so than our Heavenly Father.

Yes, in a very real way, we do worship the idols we create, the things which provide luxury and comfort but cannot provide lasting happiness or contentment any more than the ridiculous statues could for the peoples of old.

In the way we use our money we give a very accurate idea of what we worship. More money is spent in America on dog and cat food than on all the foreign missionary programs of all the churches. Whiskey, wine, and beer take more of our money than all churches or all colleges. We give God what is left of our family budgets, or most of us do. How much do you give to church compared to what you spend on yourself? This might give you some idea as to whether you put any other idols before the one true God. Yes, there are modern idols created by science, which can become our masters.

Where do you place God? First, or somewhere else down the line?

# are there other worlds to talk to?

Thou knowest my thought from afar.—Ps. 139:3

In early 1962 a convention of famous scientists met in West Virginia to talk about this farfetched subject: How can man communicate with other worlds?

Now if this topic had been suggested for scientists not

many years ago the person who brought it up might have been regarded as insane. Friends would have tapped their heads with their fingers with a knowing look.

Stretch your mind a bit, if you will. Make it work. Imagine, if you can, a universe filled with earths like our own with God's children living on them in various stages of development and advance. Here is our earth, where we have early model space ships but where half the people on the planet are still going to bed hungry at night, where war constantly looms, where over a billion people can neither read nor write. We have traveled so far but have so much to do yet.

On another earth perhaps God's children are still in the Stone Age. On another they are far ahead of us, with war, disease, poverty, and hatred a thing of the past. Perhaps they have long since taken Jesus' teachings seriously and are now living in the Kingdom he described as being within us.

Now if God has placed his children on many such planets as ours, how shall they ever get in touch with one another? That was the topic of discussion at the West Virginia conference of scientists. How indeed?

Radio waves travel at the speed of light, that is, 186,234 miles per second. This is the fastest speed of anything we know. But the fastest spaceship, if it could travel at light's speed, would take many lifetimes to reach these planets which might contain other people. If these distant cousins of ours have sent radio messages years ago they may be striking the earth now. All over the earth radio receiving stations are constantly searching the heavens, trying to pick up such messages and decipher them. Scientists are seriously seeking clues from outer space which might indicate some reasoned out system of communication. If we are sending out such messages, as we constantly are, might we not receive others in return?

All of these questions are so vast, so impossible to answer just now, that it almost seems irreverent to ask them. But surely God would not be displeased if we used the minds he has given us in ferreting out nature's secrets.

It may be that through instant communication of mind to mind we will talk with distant peoples. Mental thoughts seem to travel instantly over the miles here on earth. Will they do the same through outer space?

Perhaps our distant cousins have already visited earth and communicated some of God's secrets to us in ways we know not. Some people think so.

These questions are all so difficult, but to me, so thrilling.

How and when will we talk with God's children on distant earths? If we ever do, it will be because he, the Heavenly Father of this whole great universe, desires it.

# how long will seeds live?

A new heart I will give you, and a new spirit I will put within you; and I will take out of your flesh the heart of stone and give you a heart of flesh. And I will put my spirit within you.—Ezek. 36:26-27

As a boy in rural Mississippi I assumed that all seeds must sprout and grow the year after they were produced or not at all. Just how untrue this notion is we are learning more every day.

Through both research and accidental discoveries we are finding out some almost unbelievable facts about sprouting schedules of various seeds. Some weed seeds, for example, may lie dormant or asleep for many years in a cultivated garden or field, then come to life. Puzzled gardeners and farmers wonder: "Now where in the world did those weeds come from?" The answer—they've been waiting there years and years to sprout.

Some seeds eaten and dropped by birds or animals may wait for years or decades before sprouting. So they seem to appear from out of nowhere in somebody's garden or field.

Muskmelon seeds have grown normally after thirty years of storage. Seeds of Indian-mallow, a common weed, have sprouted after seventy years, and seeds of mimosa, cassia, and other kinds have germinated after more than two hundred years.

The seeds of Lagenaria, a gourd, have survived a year's soaking while floating across the ocean to a new, distant home. Lotus seeds estimated to be eight to twelve hundred years old have germinated.

Just how old seeds can get before losing their power to sprout we do not know. But we do know that certain seeds can live much longer than man, thus upsetting my boyhood ideas.

Seeds lose their life soonest when stored in a warm, moist place and last longest when dried out and kept in a dry, warm place.

The seeds which survive longest are those with a specially constructed shell coating, very tough and moisture resistant. Even the individual cells on such coatings are arranged differently from those on other seeds.

So after decades or even centuries of apparent death, God can bring such seeds back to life. Planted in the earth they swell, break, sprout, and grow just like they were one year old.

Likewise, our Heavenly Father has the power to change our lives, breaking hard, crusty shells of selfishness, meanness, and evil and making our lives once more attractive, useful, and lovable.

This is one great teaching of our Christian faith— that no matter how long we have been encrusted with evil, prejudice, and bad habits, with God's help we can become like new people. That's what happened to crusty old Ebenezer Scrooge in *The Christmas Carol*—life-long habits of grasping and scheming were cast off overnight when he got a good look at himself through the three dreams.

It's never too late. The thief on the cross near Jesus

Christ repented at his last hour and Jesus invited him to Paradise.

As long as we live, as long as there is the slightest bit of good left in us—which is always—God can renew our lives, changing, purifying, and making them fresh.

He brings new life to a crusty, dead-looking seed, born years before we were.

He brings new life to our sin-hardened lives and makes them once more like they should have been all along.

And it is never too late for such renewal. Like the moisture and warmth of the soil which breaks open the shell of the seed, so can the love and forgiveness of God break open the hardest human heart—if we want him to.


# God, the galaxies, and you

When I look at thy heavens, the work of thy fingers,
the moon and the stars which thou hast established;
what is man that thou art mindful of him,
and the son of man that thou dost care for him?—Ps. 8:3-4


A few faint smudges of light on photographic plates are going to affect your life and mine in a way few of us can even imagine. Such is the power of an idea.

These smudges or tiny light places on film are the photographs taken a few decades ago of "galaxies," island universes of stars like the Milky Way, of which our own solar system is a tiny, tiny part.

At first, astronomers thought there were only a few of these galaxies. But the more pictures they took through their powerful telescopes and the more powerful the telescopes became, the more the galaxies revealed grew in number until now we know there are many millions of them, each one containing millions or billions of stars much like our own sun and all at vast distances from us and from one another.

We cannot imagine the effect this discovery will have on our lives and on our descendants' lives. Only four centuries ago men found that the earth is not the center of the universe and that it moves around the sun. This astounding idea was a great shock—men had always thought of themselves as being in the middle of every-thing and everyplace. But telescopes proved we aren't. And now telescopes and scientists' minds are proving something even harder to accept—that our sun and earth are just tiny specks in a tremendously vast universe.

Furthermore, scientists tell us there probably are count-less millions of other "earths" where plants, animals, and even people like us may live. The more scientists think about the matter the surer they are that such earths and such life exist in many, many places. Now where does this leave us?

Formerly we had thought of God as having just one sun, one moon, and one earth to look after. He had just one set of children, which we call "men and women, boys and girls," to think of and love. Now suppose he has other earths to care for? How can he spread his attention and love so far? Won't people become forgotten?

The effect of these galaxies' discovery is going to be very hard on our vanity or pride. But it need not be so.

In the first place, these galaxies have been there all these millions of years and God hasn't forgotten us. Our sudden knowledge of them certainly won't change God's ability to know even how many hairs we have on our heads, the color of our eyes, the language we speak, or the color of our skin. He was our Father, a friendly Being, long before we looked through the telescope.

I have noticed that parents with one child give this child all their love. Yet I have also noticed that parents with two, three, four, five, or even seven children can give each child just as much love as the one receives. How? I don't know, but it works out that way. In the same way, God can love his human children and love his other creatures far away, if there are any, without decreasing his affection for us, and all at the same time. When I pray to him, he hears me just the same as if I were the only person in the universe. The same goes for your prayers about your worries, your fears, and your joys.

Instead of hurting our faith in God, knowing about the galaxies should strengthen it. For through the telescope we learn of a God far greater, more powerful, and wiser than the God our great-grandfathers worshiped. God hasn't changed, but our knowledge of him has changed and grown greater.

The God of the galaxies is still the God of the Garden of Eden; the God of Abraham, Isaac, and Jacob; the God of Joseph, David, Elijah, Isaiah, Daniel, Moses; and the Father of Jesus Christ. He has not changed. We have.

75617

We know more about him through our telescopes. We are like children who adore their parents, yet grow up, learn more about them, and respect and love them all the more for what they know.

To me, the pictures of the galaxies are among the most wonderful things in the world. I can look at them many minutes in wonder. They are beautiful. I know that if I travel a billion years toward them in the fastest rocket ship, they will hardly appear a mile nearer. Yet God is there in these galaxies. He created them. He keeps them going.

Is it not a truly thrilling universe we are living in—all under the control and care of one God, one Father, one eternal Savior who thinks of you and me twenty-four hours a day just as if that were all he had to do?

# *isn't the bible unscientific?*

I did not come proclaiming to you the testimony of God in lofty words or wisdom.—I Cor. 2:1

Many thinking young people are greatly bothered when they read the Bible because it seems to contradict, or go against, what we know to be scientifically true today.

For example, did God really create the world and man in just six days of twenty-four hours a day? Does the world have four corners, as the Bible states, or isn't it really a round ball? Are there oceans of water over the earth, as the Psalmist wrote? We know there aren't. There is merely air which thins out into empty space.

And you can read the whole Bible and find not a single mention of atoms, steam engines, airplanes, or any of the great scientific discoveries and inventions we now take for granted. Why?

And if the writers whom God inspired to write the Bible could be so ignorant of what every school child knows today, why do we turn to the Bible for answers to life's greatest problems?

Yes, scientifically the Bible is out-of-date. We cannot and never could use it as a textbook of science. It was not written for that purpose.

The Bible writers were not scientists either. When they used an illustration from science, they used ideas which most people believed were true. At that time practically everybody thought the world was flat. So, probably, did the Bible writers. God had not revealed to them or to anybody else the fact that the world is not flat with four corners but a round ball with no corners.

God had not yet revealed to man many other scientific truths. The atom was unheard of. Steam engines were far ahead in history.

Nobody dreamed that the earth was only one of billions of planets whirling around one of billions of suns. Even if somebody had said it was so, no telescopes had been invented to prove it.

Mankind was not yet ready to know or prove the scientific truths we know today. But certain truths about man and God cannot be discovered or proved with microscopes, telescopes, measuring sticks, laboratory experiments, or research projects. Facts about love, hate, fear, friendship, forgiveness, and prayer were well known then. God had chosen to reveal them to man even thousands of years ago.

Meanwhile, he let man discover nature more slowly. And we are finding out more rapidly than ever the hidden secrets of the universe.

Even if the Bible were being written today and were strictly in line with every scientific fact known, it would be out-of-date in twenty-five years, so fast is our knowledge changing.

Ideas which we think are true today may be disproved by evidence twenty years hence. So no Bible which is to remain true can depend on such rapidly changing notions of the universe.

The great essential facts of the Bible never change. God did create the earth, all life on it, and man himself. He did send his son Jesus Christ to earth to reveal his great love for us. He did show us how to live and love, how to forgive, and how to live as Jesus did. He did prove that our souls live after death.

These truths are more important to me than whether the atom has just one or two or ten or thirty parts.

Personally I'm glad the writers of the greatest Book of all times didn't try to be scientific. If they had nobody would read it today.

# how big is the smallest living thing?

Then Job answered the Lord:
I know that thou canst do all things,
and that no purpose of thine can
be thwarted.—Job 42:1

Hundreds of years ago, in what we call the Middle Ages, men used to debate on this subject: "How many angels can dance on the head of a pin?" The question was never decided, but it provided listeners with some interesting arguments.

Little did those men know in that unscientific age that actually many thousands of tiny plants and animals could live very comfortably indeed on the head or, for that matter, on the point of a pin—eating, drinking, reproducing, and having a gay old life.

Truly the old rhyme which goes like this:

> Big fleas have little fleas
> upon their backs to bite 'em;
> And little fleas have lesser fleas
> And so ad infinitum,

has literally come true. No matter how small an object may be, we seem to find there are smaller ones.

For with our powerful modern telescopes or even with the ordinary variety you use in school every day we can see bacteria too small for the naked eye. All kinds of them. Some useful, some harmful. Bread mold, penicillia, yeast germs—these are some helpful to man. Typhoid, tuberculosis, cholera, and many other disease germs are our enemies. They are all one-cell organisms.

We thought these were the tiniest living things. Now our powerful electron microscopes reveal to us the virus, the smallest of which is a round ball less than one ten-millionth of an inch in diameter and which causes hoof-and-mouth disease among cattle. If you enlarged a single red blood cell to the size of a twenty-five-cent piece, this virus would be a speck of dust on its surface.

Is the virus, of which there are many varieties, a living plant or animal? We don't know but it does reproduce itself, which is what plants and animals do, and which dead matter doesn't. So it might be called a living thing. And tens of millions could dwell without crowding their neighbors on a pin head! Comparing this virus with the whale, the earth's largest living animal, is like comparing a baseball with the largest star.

To me the wonder is how God can so arrange the atoms and molecules of the virus, bacteria, and whale that they all live right here on the same earth, with the virus and bacteria living inside the whale or in us human beings, for that matter, and all living right well. The more we learn about living matter the more wonderful life seems, for each peek into the small world of bacteria and virus reveals ever more complicated arrangements and processes of matter and life.

One wonders how even these tiny creatures ever get together at all. Then when we consider that our entire bodies—eyes, ears, stomach, bones, and all the rest—

are all composed of cells no bigger than bacteria, then the wonder increases.

Furthermore, the arrangements of molecules within these tiniest viruses are all perfect, regular, and exact.

How can it all be true?

It couldn't be except for a Creator, a Mind, a Being so vast, great, and wise that his knowledge and power are without limit. This Creator we call God. And he made the viruses as surely as he made you and me. Don't these tiny things make you wonder?

# has God finished making the earth?

I made the earth, and created man upon it.—Isa. 45:12

Is God through making the earth? Is the process we call creation finished? Has he stopped working on this plant? Has it stopped changing?

A careless reading of the Bible might make us think that God stopped his creative work on this old earth a long time ago, put away his working tools, and said: "There, that's done."

More careful observation of the facts gives just an opposite conclusion. God is still at work in creation. All is not done. Gigantic changes are going on right under our own eyes.

Take climate, for instance. The earth periodically warms up or gets colder. Right now we are living in a period of glacier melting. Glaciers, whether in Antarctica, Rocky Mountains, or Alaska, are melting rapidly. Ocean waters in the North Atlantic are becoming warmer.

During the ice ages all of Canada and the northern part of the United States were covered with sheets ice a mile thick. Only ten thousand years ago the last such glacier departed. Will we have another? It is quite possible.

From rock specimens collected all over the earth we know that the coldest places on earth were once covered with tropical vegetation. Not too long ago, as earth time goes, the United States was roamed by the mastodons, saber-toothed tigers, giant sloths, and other prehistoric monsters. Frozen bodies of mammoths, caught in icy bogs just a few thousand years ago, have been found in eatable condition in Siberia and Alaska.

Plant and animal life on earth is constantly changing. Various species of both evolve and then become extinct. Within the past several hundred years several animals have disappeared. In our own country only a century ago the passenger pigeon flocks used to darken the skies with their millions. Now, not one remains alive.

Lands rise and lands fall. Parts of England are sinking into the sea, with once thriving villages now visible on the ocean's floor not far from shore. Parts of our own eastern seaboard are sinking, as in New Jersey, where the beaches are being eaten away by the invading ocean.

107

Mountains, such as the Rocky Mountains, the Andes, and the Himalayas are rising. One gigantic earthquake in Assam a few years ago raised the mountains there one hundred feet.

All of these changes, plus many, many others, add up to this fact: God is still at work on this planet, creating and recreating it. Some changes are so gradual we cannot notice them, yet continued through the centuries, they make a gigantic difference. Perhaps the very spot where you live was once under the ocean and will be again someday.

God is at work in his human children, too. He is not finished with us the day we are born. All our lives we can change, grow, develop in character and soul and mind, increase in love and kindness, grow richer in spirit. Though our bodies mature early, our minds and souls may continue to thrive and increase in depth and height.

God has not stopped working on the world or on us. Growing up and growing old involves continual creation of us.

God is never finished with us or his world. Personally, I'm glad that I can change all my life and, with God's help, change for the better.

# can we ever know the secrets of life?

Then Job answered the Lord:
"I know that thou canst do all things,
and that no purpose of thine can be
thwarted."—Job 42:1-2

Man's search for the key within the key which will explain how life began on earth and how living matter can start from dead chemicals never ceases, and it is good that we seek. For in this seeking we discover facts about living matter of vast importance to our health and welfare. Every new discovery about the structure of the cell, the smallest living unit, makes medical science more helpful to us.

Some scientists say that life came to earth from some other world, perhaps on a speck of dust or a meteorite. A wandering piece of matter, they say, a part of some distant exploded planet, brought here one-cell plants or animals which gradually evolved into life as we know it. But even if this were true, what started life on that other distant planet? The question is not answered by this answer, only put off.

Some scientists simply cannot believe that a God exists and deliberately created life here. So they say something like this: Billions of years ago the sea contained just the right mixture of chemicals to produce a molecule which had the power to reproduce itself, reproduce itself again, then combine with similar molecules to make up a cell.

Now to believe that this is the way life started on earth requires more faith, really, than the Christian belief that God deliberately created the original one-cell bodies in the ancient seas with some great purpose in mind.

Consider the smallest living cell. It probably contains over a quarter million (250,000) protein molecules engaged in a multitude (thousands) of different jobs all at once, all coordinated by some mysterious control mechanism complicated beyond our wildest dreams.

Now the chances of such a cell reproducing itself by chance are so few that it would take the craziest gambler in the world to bet on it. Yet those who cannot believe in a God try to explain it as all just chance and accident. You and I, they say, are not really people. We are collections of atoms assembled for a while. That's all.

Those who believe life started by chance have their own religion—the religion of chance.

In giving his theory about how life began Isaac Asimov in *The Wellsprings of Life* says: "And if this indeed happened (and surely something like it must have), then at least once in the history of our planet, there did, after all, take place a case of spontaneous generation." How does this man know that it "must have" happened? He is asking you and me to believe life happened accidentally because he says it "must have."

Now all this sounds ever so complicated, and it is. But it is important for children to begin thinking about the subject, for within a very short time you will be faced with this question in your science courses: How did life begin?

You will have to choose in your own mind between two religious faiths: faith in God as the Creator in his own way and time and for his own purpose or faith in blind chance with no purpose.

Make your choice.

Meanwhile, every new discovery about the cell, which only reveals new mysteries, makes the faith of blind chance hard for an intelligent person to accept.

# *can we have science without God?*

The earth is the Lord's and the fulness thereof,
the world and those who dwell therein.—Ps. 24:1

Many of us do not connect God with the wonderful scientific discoveries being made every day. What, we ask, could God have to do with such complex things as atomic physics or ocean currents or the distance of stars or the way the living cell works?

What, indeed?

What connection, if any, did Henry Ford have with the Ford car? What did Thomas Alva Edison have to do with the phonograph or electric light bulb or motion pictures? Or Charles Goodyear with vulcanized rubber,

111

Alexander Graham Bell with the telephone, Guglielmo Marconi with transatlantic radio, Eli Whitney with the cotton gin, Robert Fulton with the steamboat, or George Westinghouse with the railroad airbrake?

They merely invented these great devices, that's all. They had the idea, thought how to make them work, and with tremendous patience and energy showed the rest of us how they could be useful in our everyday lives.

Strange, isn't it, that we so readily acknowledge that these men are responsible for these great inventions, yet somehow have a blind spot when it comes to giving God, the Almighty Creator, credit for knowing more than man does about what we call "science."

God, we say, wouldn't or couldn't be interested. He only knows about facts of the Old Testament days or Jesus' time. How could he be modern enough to know about rocket ships or electricity?

We don't say these thoughts in so many words, but we really do act this way.

For example, when we make some new scientific discovery, we give all the credit and praise to the man or organization or government responsible. Naturally they deserve praise but only a small part of it. For what they're really doing is using the brain power which God (not themselves) gave them to discover a truth which God made. Without him we could discover or invent nothing.

Really we often act like a little girl who sews the last button on a dress her mother has made and then thinks she's made the whole thing or like a boy who, when his father lets him put the last finishing touches on some building project, thinks he's planned and made it all.

112

Science is merely what we discover about God's universe. No more, no less. Science is about God.

The danger of thinking that we are the real inventors instead of God is that we use our discoveries for evil, wicked purposes, such as using the split atom to make war. This is not why God gave us such a great brain. No, we are to use our intelligence for good, constructive, helpful purposes, not destructive ones.

There is so much to know about this universe that we are like little boys dipping water from the ocean with a sand pail. There's always more. But it's fun dipping just the same.

Let's bring God into our learning. Then we'll be partners with the Master, the Creator, the Maker of it all.

## *how many stars are there?*

Praise the Lord!
For it is good to sing praises to our God;
. . . . . . . . . . . . . . . .
He determines the number of the stars,
   he gives to all of them their names.
Great is our Lord, and abundant in power;
   his understanding is beyond measure.
—Ps. 147:1, 4-5

I can give you no definite answer to this question nor can any man. We simply don't know, and never will, no matter how long we live, how smart we get, or how big the telescopes with which we scan the heavens.

Only God knows. It is God who is creating stars, forming new ones constantly, exploding old ones like giant firecrackers, and controlling them all according to his will.

When we view the heavens through our giant modern telescopes and through those yet to be constructed and placed in outer space where our atmosphere will not interfere with star light, then we realize how vast and omnipotent is the Being who is back of this mighty universe.

Until recently man could see only about five thousand single stars on a clear night. Many of us in our cities have hardly gazed steadily at a dozen. But until the telescope's invention even the wisest astronomers with the keenest eyes had seen only about five thousand separate and distinct stars.

Then with the invention of the telescope we discovered that the Milky Way is a cloud of stars, containing an untold number, most of them about as bright, large, and hot as our sun. Looking further, we found that our Milky Way contains perhaps 200,000,000,000 (two hundred billion) stars, is shaped like a disk, is many thousands of billions of miles thick and wide, and that our sun, located near the outer edge of this disk, rotates around its center, carrying us along with it, about once every 200,000,000 years.

Nearby our own galaxy of stars, or Milky Way as we call it, and some trillions of miles away is the constellation Andromeda, in which is a twin to our galaxy.

As if this were not enough, we have discovered dozens of other star clouds, each containing tens of billions of stars, and with the stars within them all billions of miles from one another. Scientists think that there are groupings of galaxies somehow connected and perhaps even arranged in a large disk.

As if this were not enough to stagger the mind, our largest telescopes, probing the skies, have discovered more and more distant galaxies, all containing many billions of stars, and more numerous themselves than we ever thought stars could be. We now know there are many millions of galaxies. How many? Nobody knows. As far as our two-hundred-inch telescope can see into space, indescribably farther than the human eye can reach, we see galaxy after galaxy, star cloud after star cloud, Milky Ways of Milky Ways, groups and collections of stars so vast in distance and number that they stagger any mind but the mind of God.

There is no familiar illustration with which we can make a picture of all this. Only our imaginations, straining for all they're worth, can ever begin to realize how tiny our world, our sun, our own galaxy, which we call the Milky Way, is in all this.

Yet God, who is in control of the whole universe, is not too busy to be concerned with every one of us. He knows how many are the hairs on our heads. He knows when we are sick, when we do wrong, when we pray, when we turn to him in love and devotion.

How many stars are there? Nobody can possibly say except God, but it is comforting to know that a God

115

who can create and sustain them all can also know and love us all. His power to love is as great as his power to create.

# why so many kinds of life?

And God said, "Let the earth bring forth living creatures according to their kinds."—Gen. 1:24

Rarely do we wonder about the vast numbers of varieties of plants and animals on the earth. But when we do we are amazed at the sheer numbers of kinds.

Just take some common American wildflowers—the kinds you see growing along the roadside or in the woods and fields. In America alone we have 20 species, or kinds of, gentians, 50 species of evening primroses, 250 species of penstemons, 60 species of milkweed, 50 of milkworts, 140 kinds of orchids, 15 of trilliums, 75 of morning glories, 9 of dandelions, and so on.

Of trees we have an abundance. Each of the varieties we lump together as one have many species. The oak, pine, willow, spruce, birch, elm, apple, and all the rest can be subdivided into distinct species. For example we have in the pine tree family the white, red, pitch, ponderosa, jack, loblolly, shortleaf, yellow, and others. The oak family has many families, too.

And the grasses! The grass family has so many members we won't start listing them.

The animal kingdom is just as mystifying in its variety. The snake family is large; so is the cat family, with its lions, tigers, ocelots, jaguars, and the rest.

The insect, a special kind of animal, has literally hundreds of thousands of different species, many yet unidentified, some friendly to man, some hostile, yet all with some purpose in God's world.

Each insect has its own way of feeding, reproducing, defending itself, and getting along in general. Some of these ways are so amazing they are stranger than fiction. The life of the ant is worth a lifetime of study.

Perhaps the insects greatest natural enemy is other insects or birds. If all the world's birds should die today, insects would make life impossible for man within seven years. Of birds, too, we have hundreds of varieties, each with its own way of getting along. The migratory travel of birds is a study in itself. For example, the chimney swallow which flits about at dusk spends its winters in western Brazil. The nighthawk also winters in South America.

Biologists, or students of plants and animals, have classed them into families, subfamilies, and subsubfamilies, and so on down. Someday you may learn of these divisions.

Of all creatures man has the fewest kind. Actually, we are one kind, with a difference of skin color as our main division. We have red men, white men, black men, yellow men, and brown men. Only five colors, yet the problems created by these differences of color is about mankind's knottiest problem today. In our own United States we even fought a war, the Civil War, over this question. How glad I am we don't have purple, green, gray, and other colors of human beings. The world is complicated enough now. Perhaps God in his wisdom carefully limited the colors of man, his greatest earthly creation.

Why such a variety of life? Why not one kind of universal, worldwide grass or oceanwide fish or just one kind of insect? Why? I don't know.

But the world is a far more interesting place with its variety than it would ever be with monotonous sameness.

How marvelous are the works of God! And how endless!

# did life just happen?

And God said, "Let the waters bring forth swarms of living creatures."—Gen. 1:20

It is still popular among some educated people to believe that all life, including man, was produced accidentally when certain atoms in an ancient chemically rich sea combined, then combined again, producing groups of atoms called a molecule, then this molecule and others somehow reproduced themselves accidentally until there were one-cell creatures which drifted together with other cells which became plants and animals.

All this, it is believed by many, just happened somehow and the incredible variety of life on this earth just grew and grew on its own without any Person or God supervising or directing it.

Today with our high-powered electron microscope and other fantastic laboratory instruments we are learning that even the most simple form of life, the cell, is so complicated that we are asking a great deal, indeed, of our imagination to believe it all "just happened." If you found a beautiful watch or alarm clock in the middle of the desert would you assume that the minerals of the area had somehow gotten shaken together to compose a watch or would you say: This watch was made by man in a watch factory and dropped here by its owner? Well, even the most simple form of life is more complicated by far than the finest gold watch.

For example, in a typical cell in your body, as in your little finger or in your earlobe or left toe, about ten thousand kinds of enzyme molecules are being manufactured, all controlled by an equal number of genes in the same cell. These ten thousand kinds of enzymes, or chemical liquids, are all essential to the various functions of the body and are produced according to needs of the moment.

To make one kind of enzyme—the red blood or hemoglobin molecule—about six hundred building blocks of twenty different kinds must be fastened together. It is all so complicated as to be unbelievable, yet some people ask us to think that it all just happened over the years without Anybody in charge.

In our brains there are over ten billion neurones, or nerve cells, interconnected in a fantastic system of communication, yet all contained in a space the size of a large grapefruit, retaining facts and experiences through what we call memory, so that once recorded they are never really forgotten, and providing information and experience for acting and thinking years after the facts are recorded in this semiliquid brain of ours.

Yet these ten billion cells are only a part of our nervous system which controls and regulates our bodies. Just to lift your arm to put food in your mouth calls into action dozens of muscles and thousands of nerve connections which must synchronize and work perfectly together, each doing its work at the right time. Now and then, through illness or accident, these nerves cannot work. Then we are reminded of our body's wonderfully intricate control system.

The human egg and sperm are so complicated themselves that we would hardly believe it if we could half understand. Yet, combined together, they become a teeny-weeny midget compared to the dot at the end of this sentence. But inside these microscopic bits of life are all the features of a body-to-be. Everything is right there in blueprint stage—the shape of the nose, color of hair, bone structure, toe nails, elbows, organ structure— all somehow outlined in the cells composing the human egg and sperm.

A whole library would be required to describe the human body. Yet such a library would contain only the knowledge we have now, which is only a tiny bit of what we have yet to learn.

Did we just happen or was there a God planning us? Which makes more sense?

# *how much can we know?*

How precious to me are thy thoughts, O God!
How vast is the sum of them!
If I would count them, they are more than the sand.
When I awake, I am still with thee.—Ps. 139:17-18

How much can we know about the universe? A great deal, but only a tiny fraction of what there is to know.

How much can a single person know about the universe? Only the teeny-weeniest little particle of what is known by everybody. Back less than two hundred years ago it was possible for a brilliant man like Benjamin Franklin or Thomas Jefferson to be educated in many sciences.

This is impossible today, no matter how brilliant a man may be. Each science such as physics, mathematics, botany, zoology, or astronomy includes so much knowledge that even the experts in these fields must concentrate on a special section of his field.

The total amount of scientific knowledge accumulated by the human race *is actually being doubled every ten years!* Incredible? Yes, but true. So in 1960 the world's scientists had twice as much information in books and magazines as in 1950. By 1970 we will have four times as much as in 1950 and by 1980 eight times as much. This means that no single person can today know very much about what is known, and what is known is a very small amount compared to what remains hidden from our minds, yet to be discovered.

We moderns who pride ourselves in knowing so much more than our ancestors could be mistaken. Yes, I know more mathematics, physics, and chemistry than my great-great-grandfather but I know far less than he knew about woods, fields, animals, seeds, weather signs, herbs, and lore of the outdoors. And no matter how much I know, the total my brain can learn and remember is very little indeed.

John H. Glenn, Jr., the first American to orbit the earth in space, said this after coming down: "Knowledge begets knowledge. The more I see, the more impressed I am, not with how much we know but with how tremendous the areas are that are as yet unexplored."

Even the knowledge about one single thing—the human body—is vast and complex. Therefore, we have eye doctors, bone doctors, nerve doctors, and so on. The body is too mysterious and complicated for one man to know all about all its parts. And so it is with all scientific knowledge, not to mention the facts about geography, history, art, music, architecture, engineering, education, and all the rest.

Should we tend to be proud of ourselves, we should remember Colonel Glenn and how little we really know.

Only One knows all about everything—God. Nobody else ever can or ever will. It is he that has made the sun, moon, stars, earth, and all that is in them. He understands them and us.

Each peak of knowledge is a standing place to see another such peak. When we reach that one we see two more. Get atop those and four more appear, then eight, then sixteen, all higher and farther away. We cannot climb them all, but those we can climb we should. For God wants us to.

The more we learn of science the more we learn of God—his power, his goodness, and greatness. And never worry about learning it all—we won't.

Isaac Newton, who ranks with Albert Einstein among mankind's great scientific geniuses and who lived in England three hundred years ago, wrote of the way he regarded the undiscovered and unknown universe: "I do not know what I may appear to the world, but to myself I seem to have been only like a boy playing on the seashore, and diverting myself in now and then finding a smoother pebble or a prettier shell than ordinary, whilst the great ocean of truth lay all undiscovered before me."

# is the church out-of-date?

Heaven and earth will pass away, but my words will not
pass away.—Luke 21:33

Compared to modern scientific laboratories and scientifically run factories the average church in which we worship looks small, weak, and inefficient.

Indeed, many young people and adults are so impressed by the power, skill, and accuracy of what goes on in our fantastic research centers and industrial plants that they wonder if the church has business even existing.

Many very learned persons have predicted that as we learn more and more about science we will be able to close the churches or convert them into museums. They have been predicting this for many years now.

Strangely enough the church does not seem to be dying but is becoming more and more alive. More churches are being built today than ever before and more people are attending them. True, they don't always practice what they learn, but some kind of need must send them back Sunday after Sunday. After all, no law compels us to attend and we can hold down a good job without ever going inside a church.

Perhaps the answer as to why churches haven't closed up in this age when computers can give us answers in ten seconds which would take a mathematician years to figure out is that man seeks answers to questions which don't change.

124

So a church built fifty or a hundred years ago may provide the perfect place for you and me to worship God. In it we can say: "Americans a hundred years ago sat in this same pew and prayed the same prayers, sang the same hymns, and heard the same Bible read. In this church building perhaps my great-grandchildren will also sit, pray, sing, and hear the Word of God read. They may fly to the moon on weekends, as I may fly to Europe, but when they return they will want to worship the same God as I do in much the same way."

Religion and the church somehow satisfy man's eternal needs. They satisfy his mind and soul. So the church, with all of its faults, meets an inner hunger in us all which remains the same whether we live in a horse and buggy age or in the automobile age or the atomic age or whatever ages follow in the future.

It is not the church which grows out of date most quickly, but the scientific marvels around us. Have you ever seen a picture of a hospital operating room or a high school chemistry laboratory or a factory or a textile mill of 1900? How old fashioned they appear. Even the automobiles of twenty-five years ago are called "antiques."

But a church building fifty years old, if it was built in good taste when constructed, may be considered a young church building. The church in which my family worships is exactly fifty years old and meets the needs of the people as well as it did when erected.

Jesus spoke very truthfully when he said: "Heaven and earth will pass away, but my words will not pass away."

His words of eternal truth will remain when our most advanced spaceship will look as out of date as a Model-T Ford. And where do we hear his words taught, read, and explained? In the church.

No, churches are here to stay, and will be here long after the latest advances of today's science will be forgotten.